Reverse Mortgages
for Senior Homeowners

Bob LaFay
Doris Barrell, GRI, DREI,
Contributing Editor

Dearborn™
Real Estate Education

This publication is designed to provide accurate and authoritative information in regard to the subject matter covered. It is sold with the understanding that the publisher is not engaged in rendering legal, accounting, or other professional service. If legal advice or other expert assistance is required, the services of a competent professional person should be sought.

President: Roy Lipner
Publisher: Evan Butterfield
Development Editor: Tony Peregrin
Production Coordinator: Daniel Frey
Typesetter: Ellen Gurak
Creative Art Director: Lucy Jenkins

contents

introduction v
about the author vii

Chapter 1

Reverse Mortgages: Yesterday, Today, and Tomorrow 1

Learning Objectives 1
Key Terms 1
A Little History 1
The Home Equity Conversion Mortgage (HECM) 3
How the Reverse Mortgage Works 5
The Four Basic Plans 7
Summary 8
Chapter 1 Review Questions 9

Chapter 2

A Guide to Reverse Mortgage Plans 10

Learning Objectives 10
Key Terms 10
Proprietary Reverse Mortgage 11
Government-Insured Reverse Mortgage 11
Tenure Plan 13
Case Study: Balancing the Monthly Budget 14
Case Study: Prescription Drug Relief 15
Case Study: Early Retirement 15
Term Plan 17
Case Study: Hanna and Alva 18
Case Study: Early Retirement for Aristead Brulee? 18
Line-of-Credit Plan 19
Lump Sum Plan 22
Case Study: Pay Off an Existing Mortgage 26
Case Study: Renovate or Update a Home 26
Case Study: Purchase a Condo or a Townhouse 27
Case Study: Leverage an Estate 28
Summary 29
Chapter 2 Review Questions 31

Chapter 3   **The Reverse Mortgage Loan 33**

Learning Objectives 33

Key Terms 33

The Process of Obtaining a Reverse Mortgage 33

"How Much Can I Get?" 36

The Reverse Mortgage Calculator 39

Summary 40

Chapter 3 Review Questions 41

Chapter 4   **Reverse Mortgage Expenses, Fees, and Closing Costs 42**

Learning Objectives 42

Key Terms 42

Closing Costs for a Reverse Mortgage Loan 43

Costs after Closing 47

Addtional Costs 49

Summary 50

Chapter 4 Review Questions 51

Chapter 5   **Tax Benefits and Treatments: Annuity Issues and Rebuilding an Estate 53**

Learning Objectives 53

Key Terms 53

Tax Benefits and Treatments 53

Adding an Annuity 55

Rebuilding an Estate 56

Summary 57

Chapter 5 Review Questions 59

Chapter 6   **Case Studies 61**

appendix: resource list 68

glossary 70

answer key 72

Senior homeowners are the fastest-growing segment of our population with more than 35 million people now older than 65. According to the U.S. Census Bureau, by the year 2020, senior citizens will represent one-third of the general U.S. population. Coupled with the increase of seniors as a percentage of the population is the fact that today's seniors are healthier, more financially secure, and more mobile than any previous generation. Gone are the days of receiving the gold watch and retiring to the front porch rocking chair.

■ There Are No "Seniors"

It is important to note that there are actually three different categories of "seniors":

1. The oldest (those born before 1925)
2. The middle group (born between 1925 and 1945)
3. The baby boomers (born between 1946 and 1964)

Those who are in their late 70s or 80s (or more) have lived through some very difficult times of depression and war. Their attitudes towards finance, homeownership, and retirement living are not likely to be the same as those of the next generation (the middle group—1925–1945) and certainly not the same as those of the "rising seniors"—the baby boomers.

As the leading edge of the baby boomer group moves into their 50s, their attitudes, needs, and desires are having a significant impact on many aspects of our economy. One particular aspect that relates to real estate is how this new group of "senior citizens" considers the various options available to them for utilizing the equity that has built up over the years since their original home purchase.

■ Common Ground

The family home is one area where the 80-year old and the 60-year old share common ground. For most people, the largest portion of their personal wealth is usually tied up in the equity in their personal residence. Tapping into that financial resource can be a problem for a senior on a small retirement income. Even a home equity loan may be out of reach if there is not enough monthly income to justify a lender making the loan. In many cases, the senior faced with a need for immediate funds or supplemental income has felt that the only solution was to sell the home.

■ "I Want to Stay in My Home"

Studies by the American Association of Retired Persons (AARP) show that most seniors do not want to leave their home. Half of the people older than 65 have lived in the same home for more than 20 years. Even though many of them live alone, they like it that way. They may express little or no interest in making a move even though a new, better-equipped living environment would seem to be more desirable. In many situations, seniors have paid off their original mortgage loan. "Burning the mortgage," a ritual in which the paid-off mortgage documents were literally cast into the flames, was an event they anticipated for years. After reaching such an important goal as paying off the mortgage once, it is not surprising that many senior citizens are resistant to initiating any type of new loan on the property. When there is a pressing need for additional income in order to continue residing in the home, however, there should be a way to make use of that equity buildup.

■ Introducing the Reverse Mortgage

The reverse mortgage offers an excellent solution to the need for additional income. A reverse mortgage gives the homeowner an option to receive money *from* the bank, rather than paying money *to* the bank. In effect, the homeowner is using the money that is represented by the equity in the home but is still able to reside in the property. There are three basic types of reverse mortgages:

1. Single-purpose
2. Federally insured
3. Proprietary

The *single-purpose reverse mortgage* is a specialized program offered by some local jurisdictions to assist with the payment of property taxes or home repairs and improvements. The use of this type of reverse mortgage is limited and would need to be researched through the individual's specific city or county.

The *federally insured reverse mortgage* is insured by the Federal Housing Administration (FHA). Known as a *Home Equity Conversion Mortgage (HECM)*, this mortgage may be less expensive than a proprietary reverse mortgage. It is, however, restricted to FHA loan limits determined by geographic area. Any FHA-approved lender may offer this loan.

A *proprietary reverse mortgage* can provide a larger loan amount than the FHA HECM but may also be more expensive. The choice of lenders is more limited.

■ Why This Is So Important to the Real Estate Professional

Some readers might question the value of real estate agents educating themselves on the fundamentals of reverse mortgages as seniors entering into these agreements will not be immediately listing their homes for sale. However, helping a senior citizen find a way to remain in his or her home until truly ready to sell and relocate is one of the most honorable and gratifying (and in the long run, potentially business-building) services that a real estate professional can provide to a client. The real estate agent or broker is not expected to know how to fill out reverse mortgage loan applications or calculate the exact amount that would be received under the various reverse mortgage programs. The service that the real estate professional brings to senior homeowners contemplating a reverse mortgage is the ability to understand and explain the concepts involved, to make additional informational resources available, and generally provide the personal "handholding" that is especially important for senior clients.

■ About This Book

The reverse mortgage is a time-tested program designed to allow senior homeowners to gain financial independence by borrowing against the equity in their homes. Various names are used to refer to a reverse mortgage:

- The reverse mortgage
- The reverse home mortgage
- The reverse home equity mortgage
- The reverse equity mortgage
- The home equity conversion mortgage

Because these all generally refer to the same concept, in this text the mortgage shall be referred to as a reverse mortgage, except where specifically referring to a FHA Home Equity Conversion Mortgage (HECM).

The chapters of this book concern several topics:

- The overall concept of the reverse mortgage
- The types of reverse mortgage plans offered
- Determining who is eligible
- How to obtain a reverse mortgage loan
- The costs involved at closing and beyond

Various ways to use the reverse mortgage are discussed along with examples for implementing each of the four types of reverse mortgage plans.

■ About the Author

Senior homeowner Bob LaFay was a practicing residential real estate professional along the front range of the Rockies, in the Denver metro area for three decades (1962–1992). In 1992, he became a contract instructor in the Colorado Continuing Real Estate Education Program. He developed two courses: *Home Owner's Tax Breaks* and *How To Lower Your Home Owner's Property Tax*. In 2002, he became affiliated with Alliance Guaranty Mortgage Corporation in Aurora, Colorado, as a reverse mortgage consultant.

Bob teaches *Reverse Mortgages for Senior Homeowners*, a four (4) credit hour continuing education class for real estate professionals, mortgage brokers, financial planners, and long term care insurance agents at Jones College in Denver, Colorado.

Abbreviated copy is used for one and a half hour informational seminars, which he conducts for senior organizations, community clubs, and church groups. Bob meets with seniors and their families in their homes to help them determine how a reverse mortgage might assist them in their plans to achieve financial independence.

Reverse Mortgages: Yesterday, Today, and Tomorrow

learning objectives

After completing this chapter, you will be able to:

- describe the development of the reverse mortgage;
- point out the role of FHA and Fannie Mae with reverse mortgages;
- list the requirements for an FHA Home Equity Conversion Mortgage;
- illustrate the difference between a forward and reverse mortgage; and
- name the four types of reverse mortgages available.

■ Key Terms

Collateral	Forward Mortgage	Mortgage-Backed
Equity	HECM	Securities
Fannie Mae	Home Keeper®	Reverse Mortgage
FHA	HUD	

■ A Little History

In the Beginning

The **reverse mortgage** was conceived by the Federal Home Loan Bank on January 1, 1979. Its mission was to fund monthly installments to the borrowers that would use existing **equity** in the home as collateral. The lender would receive payment for the amounts advanced in the monthly payment whenever the property was sold. The reverse mortgage was an attempt to alleviate the shortfall in a senior homeowner's monthly budget. Clearly, the intent was to provide money to older homeowners who had substantial equity in their homes but needed cash to live on. Arrangements could be made for either regular monthly payments to the homeowner or one initial lump sum payment.

Unfortunately, plan execution of the early versions of the reverse mortgage met with numerous problems and very few lenders were willing to offer the reverse mortgage as an option. One of the primary concerns was the fact that the lender was agreeing to make payments to the homeowner with no definitive date set for loan repayment. If the reverse mortgage payments should extend over a long period of time, physical or economic changes could arise that would affect the value of the property. The lender could not be assured that there would be enough value remaining in the property to repay the loan at the time the home-owner died or relocated.

ABC Lender makes a $50,000 reverse mortgage loan to the Smiths, with an agreement to make regular monthly payments to the Smiths for 15 years. At the end of the 15 years, Mr. and Mrs. Smith are moved to a nursing home and the house is sold. ABC is concerned whether there is enough value in the property to cover the repayment of the loan, plus all accrued interest and other fees. Although in most cases the property does appreciate or at least retains its original value, ABC Lender's big question is, "What if the amount that has been paid out to the Smiths exceeds the present value of the property?"

Homeowners also had concerns about reverse mortgages. Was there a guarantee that the monthly payments would continue if the bank were sold or should fail? Was it possible that the entire loan amount could come due all at once? Suppose a homeowner originated a 15-year reverse mortgage when she was 70 years old but was not ready to relocate at age 85? These questions, plus the natural reluctance of seniors to remortgage their home after many years owning it free and clear, kept the demand for a reverse mortgage very limited.

Federal Housing Administration Enters the Market

Although it was possible to apply for reverse mortgage loans from 1979 to 1989, actually obtaining one was very difficult. Without any provision for insuring the loan, lenders were simply not interested. Fortunately, help was on the way through the Federal Department of Housing and Urban Development **(HUD)**. The Housing and Community Development Act of 1987 established a Federal Mortgage Insurance Program, Section 255 of the National Housing Act, to insure home equity conversion mortgages. By providing mortgage insurance through FHA, HUD endorsed the reverse mortgage program that had been all but buried, despite its theoretical availability for the previous ten years.

On July 24, 1989, the Federal Housing Administration **(FHA)** introduced an experimental program to insure a limited number of reverse mortgages, called "Home Equity Conversion Mortgages (HECM)," with restrictions to protect both lenders and homeowners. By the time the experimental program ended six years later on September 30, 1995, HUD had pledged FHA mortgage guarantees on 25,000 reverse mortgages. This gave the program new life and credibility. Now the full faith and credit of the U.S. government stood behind the promised performance of the mortgage companies that would originate the new loans. The next step was to find a source willing to purchase these loans from local lenders.

Fannie Mae Comes on Board

The Federal National Mortgage Association, now officially known as **Fannie Mae,** acts as the conduit for money needed to fund mortgages. Fannie Mae is a privately managed stockholder-owner company that was originally chartered by the U.S. Congress to fulfill the public mission of providing low-cost mortgage funds to homeowners with low, moderate, or middle incomes. Fannie Mae does not lend money to homeowners; it buys mortgages from a national network of over 3,000 approved lenders who originate mortgage loans. By selling their loans to Fannie Mae, or pooling them to issue **mortgage-backed securities** that are then sold on the open market, lenders replenish their supply of capital so they can make more mortgage loans to U.S. homebuyers.

Fannie Mae became a strong advocate of reverse mortgages by agreeing to purchase these loans and has continued to be the nation's largest investor in reverse mortgage loans since 1989. In fact, Fannie Mae supported the reverse mortgage concept enough to create its own program in 1996. The **Home Keeper**® mortgage, Fannie Mae's adjustable-rate conventional reverse mortgage, allows homeowners at least 62 years old to borrow against the equity in their homes. The Home Keeper® mortgage is very similar to the FHA Home Equity Conversion Mortgage. The main difference is that the Fannie Mae conventional loan limits that apply nationwide are higher than FHA loan limits, set by geographic area. Because of this difference in loan limits, the Home Keeper® mortgage may make it possible for the homeowner to obtain a higher amount of mortgage loan. As of 2002, Fannie Mae had approximately 3,000 Home Keeper® loans in its portfolio.

HUD Continues To Expand the Program

HUD continued its promotion of reverse mortgages and in 1998 declared the HECM a permanent HUD program. During the period from 1995 to September 30, 1999, the number of active Home Equity Conversion Mortgages was approximately 40,000. Convinced that after 20 years of experimenting the country was ready for wide-scale use, HUD announced its intention to guarantee 1 million new FHA-insured reverse mortgages over a five-year period, starting in the year 2000 and ending in 2005. *No Place Like Home: A Report to Congress on FHA's Home Equity Conversion Mortgage Program* was the last in a series of mandatory reports to Congress on the demonstration phase of the HECM program. This report, released in October 2000, indicates several factors that could increase the volume of HECM loans:

- The costs for the loan continue to decline.
- FHA loan limits are increased.
- Public awareness of the program is raised.

With the number of people reaching their 60s and 70s increasing as the babyboomers grow older, it is predicted there will be widespread use of this major financial planning tool.

■ The Home Equity Conversion Mortgage (HECM)

The Home Equity Conversion Mortgage **(HECM)** is a reverse mortgage designed by HUD and insured by the FHA. One of the most appealing benefits of the HECM is that the loan does not have to be repaid as long as the borrowers continue to live in the home. The earlier conventional reverse mortgages were often set for a specific number of years, which could result in the homeowners' being forced to sell and leave their home before they wished to do so.

Mr. and Mrs. Senior Homeowner obtained a 15-year reverse mortgage loan when they were both 75 years old. The additional $200 per month in income has made it comfortable for them to remain in their home and pay their normal monthly expenses. At the time they originated the reverse mortgage, they assumed that they both would die before they reached 90. Thanks to good health and care, however, they are both approaching their 90th birthdays along with the termination of their reverse mortgage loan. Even if their reverse mortgage has a provision that total repayment of the loan is not due until they either die or leave the property, the $200 monthly payments will stop and they will not be able to meet their expenses. If they had a HECM the $200 in extra monthly income would continue as long as at least one of them remained at the property.

The total loan balance, which includes the amount borrowed plus all accrued interest and other fees, is not due and payable until the homeowners die or choose to relocate. There is no fixed maturity date for the loan. The HECM also provides that the total amount due to the lender can never exceed the market value of the property at the time the borrowers leave the home. The FHA insurance will cover any shortfall between the amount due to the lender and the amount received from sale of the property.

Basic Requirements for a HECM

Five specific requirements must be met to qualify for a HECM reverse mortgage:

1. Both the borrower and spouse (or co-owner) must be 62 or older.
2. The home must be a FHA-approved single-family home or one unit occupied by the homeowner of a two-, three-, or four-unit building that has FHA approval. FHA-approved planned unit developments, condominiums, and townhouses are also eligible. Manufactured homes are eligible if the borrower owns the land beneath the home and the home is permanently fixed to the foundation. Mobile homes and cooperatives are not eligible.
3. The borrower and spouse (or co-owner) must own and occupy the home as the principal residence.
4. The home must be free of debt or nearly paid off. Any low mortgage balance remaining on the home must be paid off but may be financed as part of the HECM through a cash draw at closing.
5. There are no financial qualifications; nevertheless, if the owners are in bankruptcy or are filing for bankruptcy, mortgage lenders cannot process their applications. Otherwise, there are no minimum or maximum income requirements or other financial restrictions.

HECM Counseling

One additional requirement is for the potential borrowers to receive reverse mortgage counseling through a HUD-approved housing counseling agency. The counseling is generally free of charge and must include a discussion of other alternatives to the HECM in addition to in-depth information on how the reverse mortgage operates. Upon completion of the counseling session, a Certificate of HECM Counseling is issued that is valid for 180 days. In certain circumstances counseling may be done by telephone, but face-to-face sessions of at least two hours are preferred. Because a reverse mortgage has a definite impact on the eventual estate of the senior homeowners obtaining the HECM, HUD strongly encourages other family members to attend the counseling session. Certified Reverse Mortgage counselors may be found through the HUD Web site (*www.hud.gov*) or by calling toll-free 1-888-466-3487.

Safeguards Built into the HECM Program   Thanks to the mortgage insurance provided through FHA, all of the following safeguards are included in HECMs:

1. The loan will never become due, as long as one of the owners occupies the home as the primary residence.

2. Payments will continue during the full lifetime of the surviving owner, even if the payments should exceed the full value of the home.

3. No matter how much money is paid out to the homeowners, even in the case where people outlive the value of their homes, the homeowner or the homeowner's estate will never have to repay any amount that may exceed the value of the home.

4. If, for any reason, the lender should fail to continue payments as agreed upon in the loan, FHA will continue to make the payments.

FHA insurance also protects the lender by assuring that full repayment of the loan balance will be made, even if the total amount should exceed the current value of the property. The FHA insurance premiums that are paid as part of the HECM loan provide a reserve fund to cover any losses that might be incurred by either the homeowner or the lender.

How The HECM Differs From A Home Equity Loan

The amount that may be received through either a home equity loan or a HECM is based on the value of the equity in the property. Although both the reverse mortgage HECM and a traditional home equity loan use the words *home equity* there is a major difference between the two. A home equity loan, or a home equity line of credit, requires the borrower to make regular monthly payments. If these payments are not made, the lender can foreclose on the property, forcing the borrowers to sell their home. No monthly payments are required for an HECM. Another difference is that a regular home equity loan requires the borrowers to qualify financially to obtain the loan. The ability to qualify for a loan based on income would be difficult for many seniors.

■ How the Reverse Mortgage Works

Both conventional reverse mortgages and HUD/FHA reverse mortgages (HECMs) are different from the more familiar "forward" mortgage. The **forward mortgage** is used to obtain money to purchase a home. The **reverse mortgage** is used to acquire cash. The reverse mortgage allows senior homeowners to use some or all of their home equity to address current and future financial needs. Consider the way payments are made when a "forward" mortgage loan is obtained for the purchase of a new home. As each of the 360 monthly payments is made on a 30-year loan, the principal amount owed to the mortgage lender is reduced. The majority of the payment in the early years is applied to interest. The following example illustrates how the principal portion of the total loan is reduced. (A $1,000 monthly mortgage payment may have only $100 paid towards the principal balance with the remaining $900 paid to interest.)

Forward Mortgage—$150,000 loan, $998 monthly payment, 7% interest

$ 150,000	1st month mortgage principal balance
123	1st month mortgage principal payment ($875 to interest)
$ 149, 877	2nd month mortgage principal balance ($874 to interest)
– 124	2nd month mortgage principal payment ($874 to interest)
$ 149,753	**3rd month mortgage principal balance**

When mortgage payment 360 is reached, the agreement with the mortgage lender is satisfied and the statement will show:

$ 0   mortgage principal balance

This is referred to as a fully amortized loan, meaning that after a series of equal payments covering both interest and principal, the balance of the loan will have been repaid. Most seniors have made the 360 consecutive payments and have paid off the mortgage loan on their present home. This is the starting point for the reverse mortgage.

Up the Down Staircase

With a reverse mortgage, the homeowners start back up the same ladder from which they just came down. The difference is that instead of stepping down each rung by making monthly payments to reduce the balance on an amount the mortgage lender advanced to make buying the home possible, the homeowners are now climbing back up the rungs by borrowing back from the equity that has accumulated in the home. The equity represents their accumulated savings and is actually the homeowners' own money. Recognizing that the reverse mortgage is a way to utilize the money that is currently "locked" into the home is an important consideration that may help alleviate seniors' apprehension about starting back up the mortgage ladder.

Reverse Mortgage versus Forward Mortgage

The reverse mortgage works just the opposite from the forward mortgage. With a forward mortgage a set amount is paid each month that is divided between the principal and interest due. Each month's payment towards the principal reduces the original debt. The reverse mortgage allows the borrower to draw down on the equity balance each month. It is set up as an automatic occurrence with the mortgage lender who has one of two options:

1. Electronically deposit a given amount each month into a bank account, or
2. Mail a check of a given amount each month directly to the homeowner

---

Reverse Mortgage

$	0	Starting principal balance owed on mortgage
+	350	1st month check from lender
$	**350**	**1st month principal mortgage balance**
+	350	2nd month check from lender
$	**700**	**2nd month principal mortgage balance**
+	350	3rd month check from lender
$	**1050**	**3rd month principal mortgage balance**

Interest, mortgage insurance premiums, and other fees will accrue monthly and will be added to the principal mortgage balance. As the total balance due increases, the net equity in the home decreases.

■ The Four Basic Plans

There are basically four types of reverse mortgage plans:

1. **Tenure** reverse mortgage (monthly payments as long as the borrower remains in the property)
2. **Term** reverse mortgage (monthly payments for a specified time period)
3. **Line-of-credit** reverse mortgage (draws up to a maximum amount at times and amounts of the borrower's choosing)
4. **Lump sum** reverse mortgage (total amount available disbursed at closing)

The FHA HECM only offers a lump sum payment at closing to cover the following:

■ Repaying an existing mortgage
■ Making repairs or improvements to the home
■ Financing closing costs

The HECM allows two additional options of:

1. Modified term (combining a line of credit with monthly payments for a fixed number of years); and
2. Modified tenure (combining a line of credit with monthly payments for as long as at least one borrower remains in the home).

The Fannie Mae Home Keeper® offers both tenure and line-of-credit plans plus a modified tenure plan. Both the HECM and Home Keeper® plans allow borrowers to change plans if necessary to meet their individual needs or desires. A small fee will be charged by the lender but there are no additional closing costs. This flexibility allows borrowers to:

■ switch between a term plan and a tenure plan;
■ lengthen or shorten a term payment plan;
■ add a line of credit to either the tenure or term plan;
■ convert to a line-of-credit plan from either tenure or term plan; or
■ add a monthly payment plan to a line of credit.

Combining various components of the four plans can solve both long-term and short-term problems.

> *Senior homeowners George and Mary need immediate cash to solve a pressing problem. Mary has incurred $20,000 in medical expenses that are not covered by insurance. After counseling and meeting with a lender they know their profile will allow them to draw $50,000 on a reverse mortgage. They can select the Tenure Plan for the allowable balance and spread it out to receive monthly payments for life. Or, instead of monthly payments for life, they can elect to receive the $20,000 now and set up a Line-of-Credit Plan for the remaining $30,000. This would allow them to draw funds up to $30,000 in any amount they desire at any time in the future.*

Each of the four reverse mortgage plans will be discussed in detail in the following chapters, along with examples of choices that can be made by homeowners to achieve their individual financial goals.

■ Summary

A substantial amount of the financial assets of our senior citizens are tied up in the equity they have built up in their homes. In many cases, these senior homeowners need immediate cash or a larger stream of monthly income to remain living in their homes. The reverse mortgage provides them a way to tap into that equity. Through one of the four basic plans for reverse mortgages, a viable solution can be found to meet a senior homeowner's financial needs without the seniors having to sell and move from his or her home. The FHA Home Equity Conversion Mortgage (HECM) has an additional safeguard that assures a senior that he or she will be able to continue living at home until death or until choosing to relocate with no disruption in the monthly payments received from the lender.

In some cases, a combination of two different reverse mortgage plans may provide the best option for meeting homeowners' needs. Thanks to support from the Federal Housing Administration (FHA), the Department of Housing and Urban Development (HUD), and Fannie Mae, reverse mortgages have now become a viable option for senior homeowners to cover their financial needs without having to sell and leave their homes.

■ Chapter 1 Review Questions

1. Reverse mortgages were first conceived by the
   a. Federal Housing Administration.
   b. Federal Home Loan Bank.
   c. Fannie Mae.
   d. American Association of Retired Persons.

2. Fannie Mae provides support for reverse mortgages by
   a. making reverse mortgage loans to seniors.
   b. insuring loans with FHA insurance.
   c. purchasing loans from lenders that provide reverse mortgage loans.
   d. establishing rules and regulations for reverse mortgages.

3. Fannie Mae has its own reverse mortgage program entitled
   a. Home Equity Conversion Mortgage.
   b. The Reverse Equity Mortgage.
   c. The Reverse Home Mortgage.
   d. Home Keeper®.

4. The HUD/FHA insured reverse mortgage is known as
   a. MIP.
   b. ARM.
   c. HECM.
   d. PMI.

5. To be eligible for a reverse mortgage the youngest of the homeowners must be at least
   a. 55 years old.
   b. 62 years old.
   c. 65 years old.
   d. May be any age

6. Which of the following statements regarding a Home Equity Conversion Mortgage is NOT true?
   a. The borrower(s) must be at least 62 years old.
   b. The home must be either a HUD or FHA-approved property.
   c. The home must be free of debt or nearly paid off.
   d. The borrowers must be financially qualified by the lender.

7. Joe and Mary have a reverse mortgage on their home. The balance of the loan will have to be repaid when
   a. Mary has to be moved to a nursing home.
   b. both Joe and Mary no longer remain in the home.
   c. the monthly advance exceeds the value of the home.
   d. the FHA insurance expires.

8. Which of the following statements is true when describing a reverse mortgage loan?
   a. Principal balance goes up; equity goes down.
   b. Principal balance goes down; equity goes up.
   c. Principal balance and equity both go down.
   d. Principal balance and equity both go up.

9. Bob and Jane receive $450 each month from their reverse mortgage. At the end of three months they will have accrued a total loan balance of
   a. $450.
   b. less than $450.
   c. $1350.
   d. $1350 principal plus interest and other charges.

10. All of the following are types of reverse mortgages EXCEPT
    a. tenure plan.
    b. term plan.
    c. line-of-credit plan.
    d. insured plan.

A Guide to Reverse Mortgage Plans

learning objectives

After completing this chapter you will be able to:

- list the features that all reverse mortgage plans have in common;

- explain the difference between proprietary and government-insured reverse mortgages;

- identify the factors that determine the amount to be received with a reverse mortgage;

- describe in detail the tenure, term, line-of-credit, and lump-sum reverse mortgage; and

- provide examples of how each of the reverse mortgage plans could be used to meet the specific financial needs of senior homeowners.

■ Key Terms

Adjustable Rate Mortgage (ARM)	IRA	Proprietary Reverse Mortgage
Deed of Trust	IRS Tax-Free Gifts	Social Security Benefits
401(k)	Living Educational Legacy	Special Assessments
Home Property Tax	Mortgage	

All types of reverse mortgages provide a way for senior homeowners to obtain access to the money that they have built up as equity in their homes. The principle behind the reverse mortgage is to help seniors meet their financial needs by providing cash in either monthly or lump sum payments without requiring any repayment of the loan balance until the homeowners are deceased or choose to leave the home. All types of reverse mortgages have several basic features in common:

- There are no income-qualifying requirements as the borrowers will not be required to make monthly payments.
- Title to the property remains in the homeowners' names.
- The borrowers remain responsible for payment of property taxes, insurance, and maintenance of the property. (Arrangements can be made for these costs to become part of the reverse mortgage advances.)
- The total loan balance does not become due until the last surviving borrower either dies, sells the property, or voluntarily relocates.
- The total amount due to the lender may not exceed the value of the home at the time the loan is repaid. Neither the borrower nor their heirs will be required to repay any deficiency between the current value of the home and the total amount due on the reverse mortgage loan.

■ Proprietary Reverse Mortgage

A **proprietary reverse mortgage** is one that is developed, owned, and insured by a private financial institution such as a bank or savings association. This type of reverse mortgage is not limited by either FHA or Fannie Mae conventional loan limits. For a homeowner whose property value far exceeds either the FHA or Fannie Mae loan limit, a proprietary reverse mortgage may be the best option. In most cases, a proprietary reverse mortgage is considerably more costly than one of the government-insured programs. The senior homeowner has to decide whether the additional amount received from this type of plan is worth the additional cost. The lender providing the reverse mortgage chooses which types of plans to offer, the percentage of the equity in the home that can be borrowed against, what fees are charged, and any additional requirements or limitations on the borrowers. This can vary greatly from one lender to another.

■ Government-Insured Reverse Mortgage

The Federal Housing Administration (FHA) insures the Home Equity Conversion Mortgages (HECMs) that are originated through local lenders. Fannie Mae purchases HECMs but also has the Home Keeper® program, which is insured by private mortgage insurance.

Eligibility Requirements

The FHA HECM has the following eligibility requirements for borrowers:

- All owners of the property be at least 62 years old.
- The home must be lived in as the principal residence for at least six months of the year.
- At least one of the homeowners must reside in the home at the time of closing.
- The borrowers must receive reverse mortgage counseling from a HUD-approved housing counseling agency.
- Any existing mortgage must be paid off before or at closing.
- The HECM must be a first mortgage but may be used to pay off existing debt.
- Eligible properties include single-family, one to four-unit, owner-occupied dwellings or a FHA-approved condominium, planned unit development, or manufactured home.

- The home must meet FHA minimum property standards (the HECM loan can be used to make necessary repairs).
- FHA mortgage insurance is required for the loan.

Eligibility requirements for the Fannie Mae Home Keeper® Mortgage are the same as for the HECM except that the property must meet standard Fannie Mae requirements and the borrowers must attend a Fannie Mae-approved consumer education session with a curriculum explaining how the Home Keeper® Mortgage works.

How Much May Be Borrowed

The total amount that may be borrowed with a HECM Reverse Mortgage or Home Keeper® Mortgage is based on an interaction of three factors:

1. The age and number of borrowers
2. The value of the property
3. The average mortgage interest rate

Age   In order to be eligible for a reverse mortgage, all borrowers must be at least 62 years old. The exact age becomes an important consideration in determining the total amount that the lender is willing to fund. Based on anticipated life expectancy, the younger the borrowers are, the longer the lender can anticipate making monthly payments. Servicing fees, mortgage insurance premiums, and interest are added to the principal payments made to the borrowers each month. The loan balance continues to increase throughout the life of the loan. Obviously, the loan balance will increase over a longer period of time if originated at age 62 than at age 80.

Value of the Property   The lender must feel confident that the value of the property at the end of the term of the reverse mortgage will be high enough to repay the total loan balance that has accrued. This anticipated amount is referred to as the *maximum claim amount*. It is the lesser of the current appraised value of the property or the maximum loan amount allowed under FHA loan limits for properties in that specific geographic area. The FHA loan limits are based on 95 percent of median house prices by city, county, or metropolitan statistical area up to certain limits and may change annually. Current FHA mortgage loan limits by area can be found at *www.hud.gov.*

Interest Rate   When interest rates are low, the monthly costs for the reverse mortgage loan are less and more money can be borrowed. A higher interest rate would decrease the total amount allowed for the loan. A HECM may have either fixed rate or adjustable rate interest. For HECM loans that are to be sold to Fannie Mae, the interest rate should be equal to the sum of the margin determined by Fannie Mae and the ten-year U.S. Treasury index at the time the loan is originated. For example, the lowest total loan amount that would be possible with a reverse mortgage would be for borrowers in their 60s living in a lower-priced home, when interest rates are high. The highest loan amount available would be for borrowers in their 90s living in a high-priced home at a time when interest rates are low.

Available Reverse Mortgage Plans

Five different reverse mortgage plans are available with the HECM:

1. **Tenure Plan**—Monthly payments as long as the property remains a principal residence.
2. **Term Plan**—Monthly payments are received for a set number of years.
3. **Line-Of-Credit Plan**—Draws upon a maximum credit-line amount may be made at different times and in different amounts, at the borrower's choosing.
4. **Modified Term**—Combination of line of credit with monthly payments for a set term.
5. **Modified Tenure**—Combination of line of credit with monthly payments as long as one borrower remains in the home.

Borrowers may change from one plan to another for a minimal charge of $20.00.

Fannie Mae offers a tenure plan, line-of-credit, and a modified tenure plan with the Home Keeper® Mortgage.

■ Tenure Plan

The tenure plan reverse mortgage is designed to provide payments to senior homeowners who need to supplement their income in order to achieve a balanced budget. Many seniors are locked into relatively fixed income flows such as **Social Security benefits.** Unless they also receive a private pension, many experience a shortfall in the amount of cash they need to cover monthly general living expenses.

Typically, these senior homeowners have healthy asset profiles, but the bulk of their wealth is locked into equity in their homes, which, in most cases, are free and clear of any mortgage. While they do not have to make mortgage payments, additional ongoing expenses keep chipping away at their other liquid assets, especially cash savings.

As their reserves dwindle, these individuals generally cannot refinance their homes as a source of income because they have little, if any, means of servicing a mortgage loan. A loan would require regular monthly or periodic repayment to the mortgage lender. This is not an option, as they are not engaged in regular employment.

Monthly Payments for Life

The tenure plan offers an opportunity to senior homeowners to remain in their homes for the rest of their lives while allowing for a monthly budget that covers general living expenses. The FHA-guaranteed reverse mortgage requires qualified mortgage lenders to make monthly payments to senior homeowners for as long as the home is maintained as their principal residence; in other words, until the last surviving homeowner either dies, decides to sell the home, or chooses to relocate. In the event of death of one of the homeowners, the payments continue for the rest of the surviving spouse's or co-owner's life.

Under this plan, the senior homeowners agree to use a portion of the equity in their homes in order to receive monthly payments. The advances they receive each month are secured by a **deed of trust** (sometimes referred to as a trust deed) or a **mortgage** made in favor of the reverse mortgage lender. The deed of trust or mortgage provides collateral for the loan by ensuring that the lender will be repaid when the property is sold. The use of either of the financing documents varies by state but both serve the same purpose. In either case, the mortgage lender sends a check to the senior homeowner each month, either directly or by a direct bank deposit. Once established, the monthly payments remain fixed. No adjustment is made for inflation so the amount received by the homeowner may have less purchasing power as the years go by. Other costs such as interest, insurance, and servicing fees are added to the loan balance each month, resulting in a continually growing total balance due on the loan.

The actual amount to be received each month is based upon

- the location of the home;
- the value of the home;
- the equity in the home;
- the age of the youngest homeowner; and
- the interest rate at time of closing the reverse mortgage loan.

Applications of the Tenure Plan

There are many ways that the tenure plan can be utilized to solve a senior homeowner's financial needs. Although the monthly payments under the tenure plan are less than those received under a term plan, with a tenure plan the homeowners have the comfort of knowing that the payments will continue as long as they wish to receive them. The following are hypothetical cases illustrating how the plan may be utilized. No attempt has been made to depict actual experiences from the files of senior homeowners.

| case study | ### Balancing the Monthly Budget |

Karyn Graystone was hoping to arrange for deferred payment of her **Home Property** and **Special Assessment Tax.** At her county treasurer's office, she told them her story. She and her husband Douglas were doing just fine on their Social Security retirement. They received $1,180 and $440 each month and did not owe anything on their home that was valued at $160,000. Due to a variety of physical ailments neither one could do any meaningful work, so supplementing their income could not be considered. Recently they received their Home Property and Special Assessment Tax of $2,360. And, as fate would have it, Douglas died.

Karyn's Social Security payment was then recalculated at 100 percent of Douglas's entitlement, which was $1,180 per month. She had heard of a program where the state would pay the Home Property Tax for qualified homeowners who had reached 65 years of age. She was now 69. If she could put off paying the annual tax of roughly $200 per month, and not have to pay the tax until she moved or sold her home, she felt that her budget would be back in balance. That would mean she could stay in her home for the rest of her life.

Mrs. Checkback, the county treasurer, had the unpleasant task of defusing Karyn's expectation. Many states do have this plan, she told her, and it had been discussed in the legislature of this state, but it had yet to be approved. Karyn felt her heart drop. Mrs. Checkback quickly interjected, "Have you looked into the reverse mortgage idea?"

Mrs. Checkback was able to cast some light on Karyn's desperate need to balance her monthly budget. With a tenure plan reverse mortgage, based upon the location and value of her home, the equity in the property, her age, and the current interest rate, Karyn can receive $474 every month for as long as she lives in her home with no monthly mortgage payments. Her despair could dramatically turn into elation.

| case study | **Prescription Drug Relief** |

Carlos and Juanita Perez were very concerned when they were informed that their present HMO would no longer be available in their small rural area of east Texas. The loss of the prescription drug coverage with a cap of $2,000 per year would present a real problem for them. They were both still eligible for Medicare but prescription drugs are not covered under that program. Now they would have to pay $166 per month cost of medication out of their own pocket.

Then, Carlos, now close to 80 years old, was ordered by his doctor to start taking a combination of additional drugs to address a problem with his heart. The new drugs would cost an additional $240 per month. This would make their new budget short by a little over $400 per month ($166 plus $240).

Because the Perezes own their own home free and clear, a tenure plan reverse mortgage would be a possible resource to provide sufficient funds to cover the required medication.

| case study | **Early Retirement** |

Jack and Rosamund are both 62, which makes them eligible to receive Social Security checks at 80 percent of the maximum benefit they could get if they waited until they reached 65. If they wait to retire until they are 65 years old, three years from now, they will each give up to $44,244 in Social Security benefits.

$	1,536	Maximum monthly benefit at age 65
–	**1,229**	**Monthly benefit at age 62**
$	307	Monthly loss

Both Jack and Rosamund are entitled to the highest allowable payout as they were employed at salaries in excess of the maximum Social Security scale and had the maximum amount deducted from their earnings over the years. If they waited until they reach 65, how many years would it take to get to a break-even point?

$	1,229	Monthly reduced benefit at 80%
×	36	Months (3 years from age 62 to age 65)
$	44,244	**Total reduced benefits not collected due to waiting till age 65 to retire**

$44,244 divided by $307 monthly loss due to reduced benefit = 144 months

It would take a total of 144 months, which is 12 years, to recover the monthly cost of $307. They would be age 74 before reaching the break-even point. They have calculated their financial comfort level to be $3,000 per month. Should they choose to retire now at age 62, their income flow would be as follows:

$	1,229	Jack's monthly Social Security
+	1,229	Rosamund's monthly Social Security
$	**2,458**	**Total monthly income**
$	3,000	Desired monthly income
–	2,458	Social Security monthly income
$	**– 542**	**Income shortage**

Jack and Rosamund's home is located in a suburban area outside of Springfield, Massachusetts, and would sell for about $190,000. They own the home free and clear. Considering their ages—both young at 62—the value of their home, the equity in their home, their location, and the current interest rate, they could come very close to overcoming the shortage in desired income by initiating a tenure plan reverse mortgage.

$	542	Desired income shortage
–	512	Monthly tax-free income from reverse mortgage
$	30	**Remaining income shortage**

Using the tenure plan reverse mortgage would allow them to have a worry-free retirement without having to supplement their income in any other way. If they chose to work part-time, they could do so. They would be free to take trips, visit family and children, and enjoy other special activities. According to the IRS, roughly 80 percent of U.S. seniors elect to receive early Social Security retirement. By adding the tenure plan reverse mortgage to their monthly Social Security checks, seniors can confidently anticipate a higher scale of living.

Something To Consider

As of 2000, the official retirement age for Social Security was advanced to 67 for those born in 1960 or later. Early retirement benefits of 80 percent of the maximum amount are still offered, which will put the earliest retirement age at 64. For those born between 1937 and 1960, the official retirement age will be between 65 and 67, calculated on a gradual phased-in schedule. In each case, early retirement may be taken three years earlier.

In each of the examples given above, the senior homeowners have made use of the equity in their homes to assist with current financial needs. Some seniors will still be able to work at least part-time to pay their expenses. In other cases, working may not be an option. The tenure plan reverse mortgage can provide the additional monthly income to help seniors balance their existing budget, pay for new medical expenses, or simply provide extra income as a means of enriching their lifestyle. However they may choose to use the tenure plan, the seniors can be confident that the additional income will be dispensed each month and they will be able to reside in their home for as long as they choose or until death.

■ Term Plan

The term plan reverse mortgage is very similar to the tenure plan except that the borrower receives payments for a specified number of years. The total amount of the loan is calculated the same way as for a tenure plan. The difference is that the borrower will designate how many years he or she wishes to receive payments. At the end of the designated term, the payments will stop. Although the monthly payments stop, repayment of the total balance due is not required until the death of the last survivor or upon the sale of the home. The homeowner will now be responsible for full payment of taxes and insurance without the benefit of the additional monthly income.

A Cautionary Note

It is very important that anyone planning to obtain a term plan reverse mortgage loan receive complete disclosure from the lender of all proposed terms and conditions on the loan. The loan documents must make it clear that at the time that the monthly payments stop, the homeowner will **not** be required to pay off the mortgage as long as the homeowner remains in the home. There are some nongovernment-insured term plans that do require full payment at the end of the term period. In this case, the senior homeowner could potentially outlive the period of time for which the monthly advances would be paid, leaving the homeowner in a precarious financial position and probably forced to sell the home to pay off the reverse mortgage loan.

Amount Received

The amount received under the term plan is based on the same criteria necessary to enroll in the tenure plan; the location of the home, the value of the home, the equity in the home, the age of the youngest borrower, the interest rate at the time of closing the reverse mortgage loan, and one additional factor, **the time period for which the payments are desired.**

In the following example, the homeowner has chosen a five-year term plan.

Age	Monthly Payment Life Plan	Monthly Payment Five-Year Term Plan
75	$ 550	$ 1000

Payments will stop when the senior homeowner is 80 years old. The payments are larger under the term plan because the total loan amount available is being divided over a set number of years, rather than on speculation based on life expectancy tables as is the case with the tenure plan. As long as the term plan is FHA-insured, the total loan balance will not become due until the homeowner dies or chooses to sell and leave the property.

Why Choose a Term Plan

The term plan could be a good choice for a senior homeowner who needs additional monthly income for a set period of time. In contrast to the lifetime tenure plan, it allows for much larger payouts for shorter periods, such as three, five, or ten years, at which time the payments stop although the homeowner is not required to pay off the loan balance. A term plan could be used to pay for extended home health care for a terminally ill spouse or to provide funds to finance a handicapped-accessible van. Using the extra income to offset the cost of having someone come to the home to do housecleaning or to provide personal care could enable an ailing senior to remain in his or her own home, as opposed to having to sell the home and move into a nursing home or hospice facility. Should the monthly advance available from the term plan not be large enough to cover all expenses, it will at least decrease the total that has to be raised from the family.

The following are hypothetical cases illustrating how the term plan may be utilized. No attempt has been made to depict actual experiences from the files of senior homeowners.

case study	**Hanna and Alva**

Hanna recently made the decision to move from her apartment in Sterling, Utah, to the modest farm home of her mom, Alva. An only child, Alva inherited the ten-acre minifarm from her mother many years ago. Hanna, also an only child, moved to the city where she worked at a variety of nontechnical jobs for many years. Now 60 years old, Hanna never married and spent most of her time during the growing season cultivating the land at her mom's home. It provided no income, but engaged both her mind and her heart.

Now, Alva's physical condition has rendered her unable to tend to her routine needs and reduced her mobility to a minimum. At 85 years old, she needs daily care, virtually around the clock. Alva's income was dependent upon a small Social Security check plus minimal cash derived from the sale of garden crops each season. Hanna's decision was to move into her mom's home and provide her the care she needed. She considered continuing to work using her income to pay for Alva's care, but the advantages of her personal care for her mother far exceeded other considerations. Still, there remained a need for extra income.

The term plan reverse mortgage could produce the funds to accommodate the needs of Alva and Hanna. The plan would provide monthly cash payments for an agreed-upon number of years. The amount of the loan would be based upon Alva's age, the area in which she lives, the value of Alva's home, the equity in her home, and the interest rate at the time of closing the mortgage loan. The number of years would depend on the amount of constant level cash requested for each month. Careful planning could ensure that Hanna would have adequate funds to support herself and her mother for the remaining years of her mother's life.

case study	**Early Retirement for Aristead Brulee?**

Another use for a term plan reverse mortgage would be to provide additional income that would make it possible for a senior homeowner to retire earlier. The term plan could provide monthly payments for the period between 62 and the year in which the senior would begin receiving full Social Security benefits.

At age 62, Aristead has been employed at the same store for more than 40 years. The business has been profitable and the owners of the store have set up a contributory **401(k)** retirement plan for him. In addition, over the years he has contributed to an annual **IRA** fund. Being in robust good health, Aristead's doctor assures him he will live to quite an advanced age. He is concerned about providing for himself well into his 90s. There are many things that he would like to do with his life if he could only retire now. Unfortunately, if he started withdrawing from the 40l(k) and IRA now, his retirement funds would last only 15 years. That could leave him short of income for living expenses by an undetermined number of years.

If he could leave his IRA and 401(k) that he had in nonrisk money market accounts untouched until he reached 70 years of age he would presumably be able to draw enough each month from those funds to carry him for the rest of his life. He could retire now and not have to touch his retirement funds if he could come up with $800 per month. Aristead's home is valued at $180,000 and has no mortgage, making him eligible for either a tenure or a term reverse mortgage. He is presently entitled to $1,400 per month from Social Security, based on his past earnings and his age.

Under a term plan set up for eight years, he could receive approximately the $800 he needs in addition to his $1,400 Social Security check. At the end of that period, the term plan payments would cease but Aristead's tax-deferred IRA and 401(k) retirement plan withdrawals could begin, providing him with the extra money to cover his living expenses. Assuming that Aristead understands and is comfortable knowing that the reverse mortgage payments will stop at the end of the eight-year term, his choice to retire early could now become a real possibility. As he pursues his other chosen ventures in life, he can always choose to repay the reverse mortgage loan by selling his home. Payment can be partial, or in full at any time of his choice, but is not required until he either dies or chooses to leave the home.

The ability to draw a larger amount of money for a specified number of years sometimes provides a better way to meet a senior's needs than through receiving regular monthly payments over a longer period of time. The extra money could fill in the gap between early and later retirement. It could also be used to meet short-term needs for in-home or hospice care for the terminally ill.

Seniors opting to take a term plan reverse mortgage must be careful to clarify with the lender that even though the term of years for monthly advances is shorter, the balance of the reverse mortgage loan does not become due and payable until the homeowner either dies or chooses to leave the home. A term plan that requires full payment at the end of the specified term could leave the senior homeowner in a very difficult position.

■ Line-of-Credit Plan

The line-of-credit plan reverse mortgage is an attractive option for senior homeowners who do not need supplemental income on a monthly basis but would like to have the ability to draw on funds to pay for unusual or unexpected expenses. The line-of-credit plan, like the tenure and term plans, allows the homeowner to establish a line of credit with a reverse mortgage lender based on the amount of equity in his or her home. The usual factors of age of the borrowers and location and value of the property will also affect the total principal amount available under this plan. No repayment of the loan is required until the borrowers either die or choose to leave the property.

The difference with the line-of-credit plan is that withdrawals can be made whenever the borrower wishes to do so, and in any amount up to the principal limit. This is an excellent option for someone that wishes to maintain control over the amount distributed and only anticipates occasional use. However, it may not be a good choice if the line of credit is not used very often. The expense of setting up and insuring the reverse mortgage may make it too expensive relative to the amount of cash that would be received.

Another interesting difference is that the amount of cash remaining available to the homeowner actually increases each month until all of the remaining funds have been withdrawn. The increase in the available funds is determined monthly by taking 1/12 of the sum of the interest rate being charged on the loan plus the one-half of a percent FHA annual mortgage insurance premium.

With an interest rate of 8%, add 0.50% and divide 8.5% by 12 equaling 0.71%. The cash available will increase by 0.71% that month:

Remaining $10,000 line of credit plus 0.71% increase = $10,071.51

If there are no withdrawals the next month it would increase to $10,143.53, the following month $10,216.06. This would continue until the principal loan limit is reached. Any unused portion of the allowable principal amount is not included in the loan balance and will not remain available after the loan is paid off through sale of the property.

Rate of Interest Charged

Borrowers have a choice of either an annual or monthly adjustable rate of interest to be charged on a line-of-credit reverse mortgage. (Some lenders may only offer one option.) Unlike other reverse mortgage plans, no interest is charged on a line-of-credit reverse mortgage loan until money is actually withdrawn. The rate of interest charged may vary according to market conditions. This means that the rate may fluctuate up or down according to outside economic factors. The rate of interest on other reverse mortgage plans is established upon origination of the loan and continues as a monthly charge until the loan is paid off. (See Chapter Three for a further definition of adjustable rate interest.)

The line-of-credit plan, as with all other FHA reverse mortgage plans, is guaranteed and insured by the Federal Housing Administration. The FHA guarantees the payments to the borrower and repayment of the loan to the lender with the full backing of the U.S. government.

Accomplishing Goals   There are many reasons that senior homeowners might wish to access a line of credit. As the average life span increases, retirement is rapidly becoming a period of extended opportunities. Life expectancy at the turn of the 20th century averaged around 45 years old. Today, it is beyond the 75 plus range. Retired seniors may now have an opportunity to accomplish goals that they were not able to pursue while raising families and taking care of the other necessities of life.

Using The Line-of-Credit Plan

The possible uses for a line-of-credit plan that provides instant funds with no monthly payments are as numerous as people's imaginations can make them.

Starting a Business   One such venture is starting a business. With ample ambition and plenty of time, today's senior is in a good position to realize a long-held dream of owning his or her own business—all that is lacking is money. Obtaining a commercial loan in order to start a business is very difficult without substantial assets and verifiable experience on the part of the prospective new business owner. With a line-of-credit reverse mortgage from which funds may be drawn at will, doors may start to open to attractive options.

A Combination Plan   As it is possible to combine reverse mortgage plans, a senior homeowner could draw a certain amount in a lump sum and hold the rest of the money available in a line of credit. The lump sum of cash could be used to purchase materials or enough equipment to open the business.

A retired government CPA might want to open a public accounting service. The lump sum would be enough to pay for office furniture, a more advanced computer system, a fax machine, and accounting software. Operating capital for items such as office rent, paper supplies, telephone service, and advertising could be accessed through the remaining credit line.

$	50,000	Credit line available
–	20,000	Start-up cost for opening the business
$	**30,000**	**Operating capital available**

Travel Adventures   It might be time to see and enjoy places that have been dreamed about for years. Cruises to Alaska, Hawaii, and more distant shores may now be reachable. Annual or more frequent trips can be planned with assurance that the money to pay for them will be immediately available through the line-of-credit reverse mortgage. No interest is charged until funds are drawn from the credit line. Interest is only charged for the amount used.

$	50,000	Line of credit available
–	15,000	Amount withdrawn for world cruise
$	**35,000**	**Line of credit still available to use later**

Perhaps grandkids are scattered all over the country; the line-of-credit plan opens the opportunity for regular visits. With the line of credit the money to travel around the country will be available immediately and without further worry. Funds are drawn as needed for a trip with interest charged only for the amount drawn.

Note: The mortgage lender should be notified if it is anticipated that the homeowners will be absent from the home for more than two months. If the mortgaged property will be vacated for more than one year, the terms of the reverse mortgage may require that it be sold.

Continuing Education   More and more people today find themselves embracing career changes as they cycle through a lifetime of employment. With downsizing, repositioning, and outsourcing, many could find themselves dislodged and/or unemployed. Today's seniors may find that their son's or daughter's job has been rendered obsolete and they do not qualify for any of the government-sponsored programs for reeducation. At this point in the 40 or 50 year old's life, their financial responsibilities are perhaps the greatest they will ever be. Their ability to raise money to pay for new career path education is severely limited or nonexistent.

Using the line-of-credit plan, the senior homeowner could provide the start of a new career for a son or daughter. The loan could be drawn in increments to provide funds from time to time to pay for tuition, books, computers, and so on as needed. The loan made to the son or daughter must have a provision for payment of market rate interest to the parents. The interest received by the parents must be reported as unearned income for federal tax purposes. More information on the tax liability can be found on the IRS Web site *(www.irs.gov)* or from a tax professional.

The principal idea behind utilizing the credit line plan in this way is that it provides an opportunity to dynamically employ the influence of the seniors' estate now, when there is the greatest need for money. By waiting until later when money is passed on through an estate, the timing may have passed for obtaining the benefit most advantageous to all parties concerned.

How The Real Estate Professional Can Help The line-of-credit plan option opens an excellent window of opportunity for a real estate professional to provide a special type of counseling for senior clients. The mandatory HECM counseling required of all senior homeowners considering any of the reverse mortgage plans will explain the eligibility requirements for both the homeowners and the property. The way the loan balance increases and the costs that will be involved in obtaining and servicing the loan are also covered in detail. One two-hour session, however, does not allow any time for casual "brainstorming." This is where the agent or broker can take the time to sit down with former or present clients and encourage them to throw out ideas. Reminding the client that there are no "bad" ideas and encouraging them to think of all the possible things that they could do, or buy, if they just had some extra uncommitted income can be both educational and fun! Seniors may have the idea that the reverse mortgage is only for people who are distressed and have no other recourse but to remortgage their home. The line-of-credit plan makes the whole reverse mortgage concept more one of good financial planning than one of desperation.

For many seniors, their greatest need is for additional income to meet their regular monthly expenses. For others, however, the monthly cash-flow is not a problem. Their need is for additional money to be spent on special needs or occasions. The needs may vary from personal plans for travel or starting a new business to providing funds to assist their children with unanticipated educational or other needs. With the line-of-credit plan, money is withdrawn only as needed and interest is only paid on the amount drawn. The line-of-credit plan reverse mortgage provides the senior homeowner the comfort of knowing that money will be available for whatever needs may arise and that those funds will be available immediately, without any further worry or concern, at a reasonable rate of interest.

■ Lump Sum Plan

The lump sum plan reverse mortgage is similar to the FHA modified tenure or modified term plans where one large amount is withdrawn at the origination of the loan, with arrangements made for the remaining loan balance to be paid out in monthly increments for life, or for a specified period of time. Under the lump sum plan the senior homeowners elect to draw all of the cash available to them at the time the loan is originated. The total amount available may be subject to maximum loan limit amounts set by either the FHA or Fannie Mae; otherwise, the borrowers are free to withdraw any amount necessary to fulfill their goals. Combinations may be set up, such as a certain amount of cash at closing of the mortgage loan with the balance of the loan commitment to be paid out in monthly payments.

$	40,000	Lump sum
$	300	Per month for life
or		
$	40,000	Lump sum
$	600	Per month for a period of five years

Calculating the Amount

As is true with all other reverse mortgage plans, the amount available for the lump sum reverse mortgage is based upon the same five factors:

1. The location of the home
2. The value of the home
3. The equity in the home
4. The age of the youngest borrower
5. The interest rate at time of closing of the reverse mortgage

With the lump sum reverse mortgage, all of the cash available under the individual's qualifying profile may be withdrawn at once. Interest will be calculated and charged each month and added to the total loan balance along with insurance and servicing fees. The total amount of the loan balance will be due and payable at whatever time the property is sold.

Options For Using The Lump Sum Plan: Case Studies And Examples

Helping Family Members   Some seniors might choose the lump sum option to assist family members rather than meet their own needs. For example, senior homeowners who are perfectly comfortable with meeting their monthly budget and have no need for supplemental income might have a son and his wife who want to purchase a home but lack the funds for a down payment. The senior homeowners could give the son and his wife up to $22,000 each and create what is called a "living legacy." By using part of their estate now they could benefit from the pleasure of seeing an immediate need satisfied for the family. It is an opportunity to invest solidly in their family's future.

$	11,000	Gift from father to son
	11,000	Gift from mother to son
	11,000	Gift from father to son's wife
	11,000	Gift from mother to son's wife
$	**44,000**	**Total tax-free gifts this year**

This amount can be repeated each year if the parents have the funds available. There is no requirement for repayment; in fact, there must not be any payback involved. The money must be an unencumbered *bona fide* gift. Proposals to increase the annual gift amount to $20,000 per person each year are contained in various tax reform bills. The chances of incremental increases, such as phasing up the limits over a five-year period, are under consideration by Congress.

This is a perfect opening for real estate professionals to explore creative financing for their clients. The tax laws allow anyone to make an **IRS tax-free gift** of $11,000 to another person. Although it is a fact that many seniors are struggling to meet their own financial needs, it is also true that many others are very well positioned to consider a legacy that reinforces their generosity every day for the rest of their lives. Real estate professionals are not tax experts and must be careful not to attempt to provide detailed estate planning for their clients. However, general knowledge about allowable tax-free gifts is an important tool in helping clients make decisions on ways to tap into the equity resource in their home.

Pay Off Medical Bills   In the span of just a few days medical bills can cancel a lifetime of work and seriously deplete or completely eradicate financial reserves. Family members often come to the rescue at considerable personal sacrifice, yet the ability of most children to provide meaningful assistance to pay medical bills for their parents is severely limited by the immediate ongoing needs of their own families. Furthermore, most seniors want to feel able to care for their own needs. The lump sum reverse mortgage provides a way to achieve that goal:

$	60,000	Cash available from lump sum reverse mortgage
−	40,000	Cash needed to pay medical bills
$	**20,000**	**Reserve available for future use**

Eliminate Credit Cards   According to Consumer Credit Counseling Service, as of the year 2002, the average family in the United States has outstanding credit card debt of more than $8,000. Just making minimum monthly payments of 2 percent of the balance, plus interest at, say, 16 percent per annum would require a payment of more than $300 per month. This is a sum that is quite capable of straining a limited budget. The lump sum reverse mortgage could easily address this imbalance and provide additional money by creating a line of credit with the surplus cash. No monthly payments would be required. The interest rate charged on the reverse mortgage would be considerably less than that charged on credit cards.

$	35,000	Lump sum cash available
−	15,000	Pay off credit cards
$	**20,000**	**Credit line available to be used for future purchases instead of using a credit card**

Purchase a New Car   Anywhere in the United States, possessing a reliable automobile is essentially a necessity. More often than not, older people hold on to cars that require increasingly expensive repairs as the vehicles pass the mark of their useful life. Justifying the purchase of a new or newer model may not require much contemplation. As an extra layer of security it could alleviate much inner fear of incurring expensive repairs or being stranded in a broken-down car.

$	30,000	Cash available from lump sum reverse mortgage
−	20,000	Cash needed to purchase a new car
$	**10,000**	**Cash reserve available for future use**

Living Educational Legacy   A **living educational legacy** to help grandchildren attend college is gaining in popularity. Most states now offer prepaid college plans that call for the payment of a sum of money today to the university or college selected. In return the educational institution will guarantee that the student for whom it is intended will be able to attend the selected college or university. This of course depends on the prospective student's possessing the proper credentials such as a high school diploma, satisfactory grades, and adequate SAT scores. The tuition is based upon today's fees and does not increase in the future.

$	50,000	Lump sum available
–	50,000	Prepaid tuition to college or university
	0	**Amount owed at matriculation**

No federal tax is owed by senior homeowners who obtain funds through a reverse mortgage. Furthermore, the prepaid tuition does not come under the annual gift tax limits of $11,000 per person. The parents of the grandchild are not taxed, nor is the grandchild. In contrast, receiving a direct gift from the grandparents could cause a taxable event if the amount exceeded $11,000 from each grandparent. Tuition and fees prepaid to universities or colleges are tax free.

College educational costs, both tuition and other ancillary costs, such as books, materials, etc., have far outpaced the national rate of inflation in recent years. Therefore, the reverse mortgage is potentially a good hedge against inflation.

Senior homeowners who are financially secure may want to explore the exciting possibilities of a living educational legacy. Grandparents can assure financial stability for one or more of their grandchildren and hopefully gain the satisfaction of seeing their dreams fulfilled. It is a living gift that engages a piece of the future today.

The following examples are hypothetical and no attempt has been made to depict actual experience from the files of senior homeowners.

| case study | **Pay Off an Existing Mortgage** |

Mayli Wong is 67 years old and owns the home that is her principal residence. She has an outstanding mortgage of $42,000 that requires a monthly payment of $300 to principal and interest. Her home is valued at $135,000. She and her husband, Lee, had lived in the home outside of Eugene, Oregon, for more than 20 years until they retired last year. They both receive Social Security checks and were able to balance their financial needs each month. When Lee became adamant about selling their home and moving back to his family home in Taiwan, Mayli said, "Go"... and he did, after signing his interest in the home over to her.

Now Mayli is unable to work due to extreme arthritis in both hands. Her sole source of income is her Social Security check of $950 per month. She has few bills but needs more monthly income. She feels that she could balance her monthly budget if she did not have the mortgage payment each month. She would not be able to qualify for a home equity loan because she has no means of repayment. The lump sum plan reverse mortgage could provide enough funds to pay off her mortgage, plus pay for all related closing costs and funding fees. The advantages for Mayli would be that:

- she would be able to live in her home free of the existing mortgage payment;
- she could live in her home the rest of her life and never have to move;
- she would be free of worry as she would not have to use her savings, if any, to make monthly mortgage payments; and
- she would not have to sell her home, which might become necessary if she does not eliminate the $300 per month shortfall in her budget.

In the event that Mayli gets sick and incurs medical bills in excess of her medical coverage, she will have a layer of protection against enforceable liens. Without the reverse mortgage, the liens for unpaid bills could perhaps be large enough to equal or exceed the equity she has in her home. In this case, the liens could become a judgment that could eventually force foreclosure. With a reverse mortgage, it is doubtful that a judge would order immediate payment of the current bills.

case study	**Renovate or Update a Home**

Talking with her brother Gary after dinner at her home in Mobile, Alabama, one night, Rene brought up the subject of their mom and dad. She had been worrying about how high utility bills might be affecting their parents' pocketbook. The parents live in a 60-year-old bungalow in a small town near Niagara Falls in upstate New York. They bought their home nearly 40 years ago and it has never been adequately insulated. Gary shared Rene's concern, but said that he felt that their parents did not have the money to have the work done. Rene, sensing that she had hit a responsive chord, quickly added, "No, and neither one of us can afford to have it done for them." Relieved that they both perceived the situation at the same level, Gary added what he thought was a final sentiment. "I would love it if we could do something to help them make ends meet, but…." What Rene had in mind was much more ambitious.

Rene asked her brother, "What would you think of approaching them with the idea of a complete updating of their home?" Gary liked the idea but pointed out that the old couple could not go into debt. In fact, their retirement money was just barely adequate for their needs. Rene had prepared a list of improvements, along with estimates, which could reduce their cost of living and add a lot to their enjoyment. The total for new insulation, storm windows and doors, lifetime siding, a new heating and cooling system, new kitchen appliances, and complete painting and new carpet throughout the house came to $29,700.

Rene then explained to Gary that with their parents' home valued at $125,000, clear of any present mortgage, and with both of them being 70 years old, they could easily qualify for a lump sum reverse mortgage. The value of their home would increase because of all of the improvements and this could all be accomplished without requiring any money out of their pockets. Gary's last comment was, "OK, Rene—let's go talk to the folks!"

case study	**Purchase a Condo or a Townhouse**

Another option for using the lump sum plan reverse mortgage would be beneficial financially to the real estate professional as well as to the senior homeowner. The lump sum plan has the flexibility to serve as a conduit to solving a more complex consideration such as selling an existing home that has become a burden and moving into a different type of living arrangement. In this way, the seniors would be able to live more comfortably in a home that was better suited to their needs as they grow older. The real estate professional could assist them in the sale of one property and the purchase of another.

Thirty-seven years ago the Overlooks bought a modest three-bedroom ranch home in a suburb of Oklahoma City where they raised their family of two boys and one girl. For years, Bud prided himself on having the best-looking landscaping on the block, cutting and manicuring the lawn twice each week. As the years went on, however, he experienced problems with his right hip. The pain was substantial, but getting a lawn service to tend to the grounds was cost prohibitive. Finally, Bud had to have the hip replaced and cutting the grass or shoveling snow became impossible for him. The Overlooks' children, now all adults with their own families, had moved to other locations around the country, so asking them for help was out of the question.

The next-door neighbor, George, a real estate broker, suggested they look into selling the house and buying a condominium where no lawn or house maintenance would be required. He even brought over a brochure for a new project being built nearby. Much as the idea appealed to them, they were reluctant to even consider making a move in that direction. George told Bud that he and his wife, Emily, had recently taken out a reverse mortgage on their home. Perhaps this would be a solution for the Overlooks?

Bud, after hearing the details on reverse mortgages, said it would not work for them. As more conversation took place, George discovered the reason for Bud's reluctance. He had refinanced his home to help his children attend college and still owed about $40,000. By his calculations, even if he did sell his house, he would be about $40,000 short of having enough money to pay off the present mortgage and purchase the condominium. At his age of 77, with no employment, he felt that no lender would ever extend a loan to him. George, based on his years of real estate experience, told Bud to "never say never." George was confident that there was a way to use the reverse mortgage plan to help the Overlooks move into the new property.

George suggested that Bud and his wife, Jerrie, put their home up for sale for $150,000 and then prepare an all-cash offer for a one-bedroom unit at the Riverview Adult Condominium Community. The offer was made with a dual contingency; one contingency subject to the sale of their current home, and the other subject to their obtaining a reverse mortgage on their new condominium. Sale of the present home provided the cash to purchase the condominium outright so they could own it free and clear of any mortgage loan. They could then place a lump sum reverse mortgage on the new property, providing them with the money to pay off the existing $40,000 loan on their old home, plus enough to cover all of the reverse mortgage loan origination costs. Settlement on both properties plus settlement on the reverse mortgage would have to occur consecutively. It was a complicated transaction, but one that would allow them to live mortgage-free for the rest of their lives, in a community they would enjoy and where they would have no concerns about maintaining the home. The Overlooks are very proud of their new home—and thankful to their neighbor and real estate broker. George is happy to have been able to help his neighbors move to a new lifestyle—and, of course, for achieving both a listing and a sale!

A real estate professional can work with a reverse mortgage lender to prepare an analysis of an individual's financial profile and compile all of the paperwork details that will be involved. Together they can custom-design a package similar to the Overlooks' example, or explore other options. This is a powerful team approach and provides a high degree of confidence and trust for the senior homeowner as the financial plan is explained and implemented.

case study   **Leverage an Estate**

Maria and Ernesto Perez were talking with friends one night at their home in Oak Park, Illinois. Out of nowhere, Maria asked if anyone ever thought about getting rich. Ernesto kept his own counsel as he was still trying to recover from an ill-timed funds investment. Maria pushed on with her vision. Their friends, Sam and Lynn Dustin, responded instantly with "not at our age." All four of the friends were retired, in their mid-60s. They felt secure with Social Security checks each month, plus modest retirement plans. They also had covered catastrophic medical contingencies with Medi-Gap insurance, and as an extra precaution, had long-term care insurance.

Maria told them she had attended a class at the senior center and had learned about reverse mortgages for seniors. Ernesto took exception to the suggestion of a mortgage, as their home was now free of debt. She responded, "Wait, what I'm talking about is multiplying our estate, to leave more to our children." Seeing she was serious, his opposition started to shift to wonderment. "How could we do that?" was the unspoken question. Maria began to unravel the answer. She told them she would like to share with them what she had learned in the class about a plan that was called "Leveraging Your Estate."

It seems that after the session on reverse mortgages, Harry Bachzerkel, one of the members at the senior center, asked people to stay to participate in a PowerPoint presentation on alternative uses of the reverse mortgage. Maria responded to his request for someone to provide information to use as a model. He had a laptop computer hooked up to a screen projector and made entries using what he called the reverse mortgage calculator. Based on the information Maria gave him, he came up with this example:

$ 175,000	Market value of the home
Age of the senior homeowners	65, 66
Location by zip code	60300
$ 60,000	**One lump sum available**

Harry had entered the market value of the Perez' home, their age, and the zip code. The obtainable result that came up was $60,000 cash in one lump sum. Harry suggested that they use $30,000 of the amount as a down payment on a single-family home that they would own as a rental investment.

$ 150,000	Market value
– 30,000	Down payment
$ 120,000	Mortgage loan @ 7% fixed rate interest, 20-year term
$ 1,800	Annual real estate tax
$ 600	Annual home insurance

To determine the total monthly payment on the rental property, Harry invited them to log on to the Consumer News Systems Web site. He told them that there is no charge of any kind for using this site, *www.cnsweb.com.* By entering six items of information the computer will calculate the total monthly payment.

$	120,000	Loan amount
$	150,000	Appraised value
Term in years	30	
Interest rate	7%	
$	1,800	Yearly property tax
$	600	Yearly property insurance
$	**998.36**	**Total monthly payment**

Harry further advised those who were seriously interested to move in the direction of selecting a professional team to help them achieve their goals. He suggested that the team be made up of:

- A REALTOR® who understands the goal to be accomplished and will work to help in achieving it.

- One or two mortgage lenders. A mortgage lender will be needed to originate the loan for the home purchase investment and concurrently a lender will be needed to initiate the reverse mortgage.

The two events have to be synchronized; one cannot take place without the other. The reason two mortgage lenders may be needed is that there are a limited number who make reverse mortgages. If one lender can handle both transactions, that is better. If not, then coordination is required and that is where the real estate professional's services come to the rescue. The REALTOR® can assist in setting up the whole loan process and also in locating investment properties.

It is important to remember that investment property requires management. This can be done by the senior who has plenty of time and energy. It can also be handled by professional management companies but that will, of course, cost money.

One additional note regarding whether leveraging an estate is a valid concept is to find out how much home prices have actually increased over the past 20 years in the senior homeowner's particular geographic area. The Consumer News Systems Web site *(www.cnsweb.com)* provides this information. A comprehensive listing of all 50 states and the District of Columbia, listed in order of highest to lowest increase over a 20-year period, can be found on this site. This figure can be divided by 20 to arrive at an average annual increase.

■ Summary

Although private lenders do offer proprietary reverse mortgages, the most popular type of reverse mortgage is the FHA-insured Home Equity Conversion Mortgage. FHA-insured mortgages are often sold to Fannie Mae. The amount that can be borrowed with a HECM is based on the age and value of the property plus the interest rate that can be charged for the loan.

There are four basic types of reverse mortgages: 1. the tenure plan, which provides equal monthly payments for life (or for as long as at least one homeowner remains in the property); 2. the term plan, which provides for payments for a set number of years; 3. the line-of-credit plan, which allows the borrowers to draw down funds at any time and in any amount up to the established limit; and 4. the lump sum plan where the borrowers take the full amount available in one lump sum at settlement.

Of the four types of reverse mortgages that are available—the tenure plan, term plan, line-of-credit plan, and lump sum plan—the lump sum appears to offer the most variety of ways to make use of the equity build-up present in many seniors' homes. The lump sum payout can be used to provide financial assistance or improve the lifestyle of the seniors themselves. It can also be used in numerous ways to benefit their children. In many cases, being able to provide financial assistance at a time when their middle-aged children are at the peak point of their own financial obligations, is more appealing than leaving the money to them years later after the parent's death.

Another possible use for a lump sum reverse mortgage is for the senior homeowners to leverage their own estate. Careful study of current market conditions and utilization of a team of professionals is very important for seniors choosing to embark on this particular investment path.

Whatever the motivation for obtaining a reverse mortgage, the funds received provide the senior homeowner a large block of cash that requires no monthly payments and does not require repayment until the borrowers are either deceased or have chosen to leave the property. When the house that serves as collateral for the loan is no longer maintained as the senior's principal residence, the property must be sold and the money received from the sale pays off the total amount due on the reverse mortgage. Any funds received in excess of the amount due the reverse mortgage lender are distributed either to the senior homeowners or to their heirs.

■ Chapter 2 Review Questions

1. The tenure plan reverse mortgage provides for
   a. monthly advances for a set number of years.
   b. monthly advances for life, or until the homeowners leave the home.
   c. monthly advances that vary in amount according to inflation.
   d. monthly advances until one of the married homeowners dies.

2. The advances received by the homeowner through a reverse mortgage are secured by a
   a. promissory note.
   b. deed of trust or mortgage.
   c. FHA insurance.
   d. Fannie Mae Mortgage Backed Security.

3. The actual amount that will be received each month depends on all of the following EXCEPT
   a. location of the home.
   b. equity in the home.
   c. market value of the home.
   d. financial ability of the homeowners.

4. With a tenure plan reverse mortgage, each month the lender
   a. sends a check to the homeowners or makes a deposit to their account.
   b. makes payments to designated creditors in the homeowners name.
   c. establishes a line of credit to be drawn upon at will.
   d. deposits the monthly advance in the homeowners' IRA account.

5. Bill and Mary obtained a reverse mortgage in 2000. When Bill died unexpectedly in 2002
   a. Mary was forced to sell the home.
   b. Mary had to pay off the lender in order to stay in the home.
   c. Mary's family had to provide funds to pay off the loan.
   d. Mary's monthly advances from the lender will continue until she either dies or decides to leave the home.

6. With a term plan reverse mortgage, the homeowner will receive
   a. larger monthly advances for life.
   b. larger monthly advances for the specified term of years.
   c. one lump sum payment at the beginning.
   d. an established line of credit.

7. The one additional factor that must be taken into consideration with a term plan reverse mortgage is the
   a. credibility of the homeowners.
   b. state of health of the homeowners.
   c. time period for which payments are desired.
   d. the projected life span of the homeowner.

8. The term plan might be the best solution in which of the following cases?
   a. Carlos's wife has diabetes and will require expensive medication daily.
   b. Helen's husband has terminal Lou Gehrig's disease and needs hospice care.
   c. The Lees have agreed to raise their three year-old granddaughter and will have more monthly expenses.
   d. The cost of oil has increased to where the Duncans pay double what they did before for heating.

9. The line-of-credit plan reverse mortgage differs from the tenure or term plan in that
   a. monthly advances are made for life.
   b. monthly advances are made for a set number of years.
   c. funds are withdrawn only when needed.
   d. funds are withdrawn on a monthly basis.

10. Interest is charged on the line-of-credit plan
    a. based on the total amount available.
    b. as money is withdrawn.
    c. based on an anticipated monthly withdrawal.
    d. at the end of the term.

11. Robert and Marie love to travel around the country. They need to be aware that
    a. the mortgage lender should be notified if they plan to be away from home more than one month.
    b. they will only be able to withdraw funds from the line of credit in their hometown.
    c. they will be limited in the amount they can withdraw when away from home.
    d. the lender may force sale of the property if it is vacated for more than one year.

12. Helene has decided to withdraw $40,000 to pay off her mortgage and receive $300 per month for the rest of her life. This is an example of a
    a. tenure plan.
    b. term plan.
    c. combination lump sum and tenure plan.
    d. combination lump sum and line-of-credit plan.

13. George and Miriam would like to use the funds from their lump sum reverse mortgage to make a gift to each of their two granddaughters. The maximum each girl could receive under the IRS gift law would be
    a. $ 5,500
    b. $11,000
    c. $22,000
    d. $44,000

14. Robert has established a living educational legacy for his grandson Tim by using a lump sum reverse mortgage to pay for a prepaid tuition plan at a selected college. Which of the following statements is NOT true?
    a. The college will have to accept Tim regardless of his grades.
    b. The prepaid tuition does not fall under the $11,000 gift tax limit.
    c. Tim will not have to pay income tax on the amount.
    d. Tim's parents will not have to pay unearned income tax on the amount.

15. Some seniors today are actually able to use a reverse mortgage to buy a new home such as a condominium where no maintenance will be required. The contract for purchase of the new home *must* be made contingent on the
    a. approval of their daughter and son-in-law.
    b. sale of their current home plus the ability to secure a reverse mortgage loan on the new property.
    c. replacement of all equipment in the condominium unit.
    d. inclusion of a homeowner's warranty on the appliance.

The Reverse Mortgage Loan

learning objectives

After completing this chapter, you will be able to:

- explain the importance of reverse mortgage counseling;

- locate a reverse mortgage lender;

- list important things to consider in selecting a lender;

- describe in detail the factors involved in determining the amount available for a reverse mortgage loan; and

- discuss the factors affecting the total loan amount available.

■ Key Terms

Fannie Mae Loan Limit	Maximum Claim Amount	Origination Fee
FHA Loan Limits	NRMLA	Servicing Fee

■ The Process of Obtaining a Reverse Mortgage

Because the entire concept of the reverse mortgage is so different from that of a forward mortgage it is extremely important that adequate time be given to senior homeowners for them to absorb and understand fully each of the steps to be taken. Time should be allowed to review the way loan documents and monthly statements will appear. A government-insured reverse mortgage requires certified counseling and HUD-approved lenders.

Obtaining Counseling

Both the FHA Home Equity Conversion Mortgage (HECM) and the Fannie Mae Home Keeper® require that all potential reverse mortgage borrowers attend at least a single two-hour counseling session with a HUD-approved reverse mortgage counselor before applying for a reverse mortgage. The counseling focuses on the difference types of HECMs and discusses different alternatives to obtaining a

HECM. The purpose of the counseling is to help the senior homeowner decide if a HECM is the most appropriate way to meet financial needs. If face-to-face counseling is not possible, it is possible to make arrangements for counseling by telephone.

Upon completion of the counseling session, the prospective borrower is given a Certificate of HECM Counseling. This certificate is valid for 180 days and must be presented to the reverse mortgage lender at the time of application. If the reverse mortgage loan is not closed within that time period a renewal certificate must be obtained. Renewal is generally granted without any requirement for additional counseling.

Locating a Lender

There are authorized FHA and Fannie Mae lenders in all areas of the country. A general list of lenders offering FHA Home Equity Conversion Mortgages (HECM) can be found through the HUD Web site at *www.hud.gov.* The Fannie Mae Web site, *www.fanniemae.com,* lists lenders that offer both the HECM and the Fannie Mae Home Keeper®. HECM lenders are also listed on the American Association of Retired Persons Web site, *www.aarp.org.*

Some private proprietary reverse mortgage lenders in the marketplace are backed by the resources of the mortgage holder and/or private insurance company. A list of available lenders for both government-insured and proprietary reverse mortgage lenders can be accessed on the Web site of the **National Reverse Mortgage Lenders Association (NRMLA)** at *www.reversemortgage.org.* According to NRMLA, the lenders members of this organization make more than 90 percent of all the reverse mortgage loans in the United States.

Although reverse mortgage lenders are located throughout the country, it is possible there might not be one at a location convenient for a senior homeowner to make application. This situation would provide an opportunity for a real estate professional to assist the senior client by either taking the client to the nearest lender's office or agreeing to transport paperwork back and forth on behalf of the senior. In some cases the application can be taken over the telephone; nevertheless, the Certificate of HECM Counseling must be delivered to the HECM lender.

Factors To Consider in Selecting a Lender

Costs   The only costs that lenders actually control are the origination fee and the servicing fee. The **origination fee** is a fee charged by the lender to cover the cost of preparing the loan application and processing the loan. The **servicing fee** is a flat fee that is added to the loan balance each month that covers the costs of record keeping involved in processing the loan advances and mortgage insurance premiums. Both FHA HECM and Fannie Mae Home Keeper® origination fees are limited to a charge of 2 percent of the maximum claim amount or $2,000, whichever is greater. The **maximum claim amount** is the highest amount that the lender can collect at the time the property is sold, regardless of the total loan balance due at that time. The servicing fee is determined by the lender but may not exceed $30 per month for an annually adjusting interest rate, and $35 per month for a monthly adjusting interest rate.

Third-party closing costs for services and charges such as appraisal, credit report, title report and insurance, inspection fees, and recording fees, seldom vary much from one lender to another but will vary from one locality to another and should be fully disclosed along with the amount charged for origination and servicing. All closing costs may be financed as part of the reverse mortgage loan. If the lender requires that fees for appraisal, inspections, or other services provided by a third party be paid in cash at the time of application, these fees may be reimbursed to the borrower at closing and added to the loan balance.

In the case of a proprietary reverse mortgage, the interest rate charged on the loan will be determined by the private lender. The FHA Home Equity Conversion Mortgage (HECM) interest rates are subject to change every week; in any given week, however, all lenders will charge the same interest rate on a HECM loan. The HECM interest rate is tied to the one-year U.S. Treasury Security rate published daily in the *Wall Street Journal, USA Today*, and other major newspapers. The Home Keeper® interest rate is based on the current weekly average of the secondary market Certificate of Deposit Index plus a margin determined by Fannie Mae. Both the HECM and Home Keeper® loans have specific limits on both the annually adjusting and monthly adjusting rates. These limits are not under the control of any individual lender.

A change in the interest rate charged on a reverse mortgage loan has no effect on either the amount or the number of payments made to the senior homeowner. It does affect the total loan balance due, however. An increase in the interest rate would cause the loan balance to grow faster; a decrease in the interest rate would slow down the growth of the total loan balance.

Experience   The more knowledge senior homeowners have about the entire reverse mortgage plan, the better they will be able to judge how well a prospective lender understands this product. A lender who has placed many reverse mortgage loans will be better prepared to handle any unexpected snags or problems along the way. Moreover, a lender who handles a number of HECMs each year is likely to have a good working relationship with the local HUD office, which may make the process go more smoothly. It is very important that the individual loan officer preparing the loan application, as well as the processor who will compile the paperwork necessary and the lending company as a whole, are familiar with the entire reverse mortgage process and have a track record of successful completions of this special type of mortgage loan product.

Servicing: Administrative Functions after the Loan Has Closed
Servicing refers to the handling of administrative functions after a loan is closed. If a lender originates only a few reverse mortgage loans per year, that lender may decide to transfer the loans to another office or company specializing in reverse mortgage loans. By their very nature reverse mortgages are much more complicated that the typical "forward" mortgage. With a forward mortgage used to purchase a home, the lender loans an agreed-upon amount to the borrower at closing. The loan agreement establishes the exact amount that is to be paid back to the lender each month. After a certain number of payments the loan is paid off and the agreement is complete. The servicing in this case would be limited to ensuring tax and insurance premiums are timely paid and that payments are received monthly from the borrower and properly credited to the right account. In the case of an adjustable rate mortgage, extra calculations would need to be made at each adjustment period.

With the tenure, term, and lump sum reverse mortgages the principal amount of the loan would be established for regular additions to the outstanding loan balance. The charges for interest, insurance, and servicing are additional and must be calculated into the total loan balance each month. The line-of-credit plan is the most complicated as the interest is not charged until withdrawals are made and the principal amount available may actually increase over the term of the loan.

The amount charged for servicing the loan may vary from one lender to another although the HECM and Home Keeper® do have certain restrictions.

The real estate professional may want to suggest that the client request a sample copy of how account statements will appear each month. This is especially true in the case of a line-of-credit reverse mortgage where the amount of available credit may actually be increasing over time. In most cases, the senior homeowners will not have been reviewing any type of mortgage loan statements for a number of years. Because the style of monthly and annual statements varies greatly from lender to lender, this is an opportunity for the real estate agent to be involved by helping the homeowner understand what each monthly statement means and to seek more information about any points that are not clear.

Commitment   Professional commitment to meeting the consumers needs can sometimes be seen in the lender's professional relationships. Members of the National Reverse Mortgage Lenders Association (NRMLA) have developed a set of "best practices" to be used in working with reverse mortgage customers. In the same way that a real estate professional may point out his or her affiliation with the National Association of REALTORS® or a professional designation such as Certified Real Estate Specialist to gain credibility in the eyes of the client, the members of the NRMLA see the association as one that assures the loan applicant of a higher standard of treatment. Not all lenders are interested in making the extra effort involved in originating a reverse mortgage loan. As the amount of the loan is based on a percentage of the value that is expected to remain with the home at the time the loan balance is paid off, in many cases the amount of the loan is rather small compared with loans originated for purchasing a home. Lenders who dedicate a part of their portfolio of loans to reverse mortgages show a genuine interest in, and concern for, their elderly clients.

■ "How Much Can I Get?"

This has to be the number one question in most seniors' minds as they think about how the reverse mortgage might help them gain, or retain, financial independence. In this section, many of the most likely questions will be addressed. The constant state of change that is a part of the nature of life makes the amount available for a reverse mortgage loan a moving figure—not a simple set answer. Several important factors affect the amount that will be available.

Location

"Location, location, location" is the watchword of the real estate industry and applies to the reverse mortgage to the same degree as for the traditional forward mortgage. The location of the home is usually the primary factor for determining the value of the property. The exact same exterior and interior design of a house may vary by thousands of dollars in market value depending on where it is located within a city, county, or even state. Even in tract housing, where all of the models are virtually the same, the value of one house will vary from another due to its location near the school, a park, public transportation, or a busy street. In the case of senior homeowners who have lived in the same property for many years, the value may have escalated tremendously as a result of economic changes within the community. On the other hand, an encroaching highway or commercial business may have reduced the value of the property since the homeowners first purchased it.

Market Value

The market value of the home at the time of closing the reverse mortgage loan will determine the maximum claim amount that a lender can make at the time the reverse mortgage ends and the total loan balance is paid. The amount available to the homeowner is based on a percentage of this amount, taking into consideration the age of the borrowers and current interest rates. The lender may request that a certified appraisal be made at the time of loan application to determine the value. If the homeowner is seeking a FHA HECM loan the market value cannot exceed the FHA loan limits that are set by specific geographic area. The Home Keeper® loan value must stay within the **Fannie Mae** (conventional) **loan limit.**

Loan Limits

FHA loan limits are determined by taking 95 percent of the average house price in a specific city, county, or metropolitan area. The 95 percent figure is then subject to limits ranging from $154,896 in standard areas up to $280,749 in high-cost areas (Year 2003 limits). Properties in Alaska, Hawaii, and the U.S. Virgin Islands are 50 percent higher as a result of increased costs of building and higher sales prices. The limit may change at the beginning of each year depending on average house prices. There is legislation proposed in Congress to allow FHA maximum loan limits to apply uniformly in all areas of the country as is the case with conventional Freddie Mac and Fannie Mae loans.

The Home Keeper® loan is subject to the Fannie Mae (conventional) loan limit that is subject to change each year based on average loan commitments. The 2003 limit is $322,700. Higher loan limits are available through private, non-FHA insured proprietary reverse mortgages in some areas. Both FHA and Fannie Mae reverse mortgages are available in all 50 states and the District of Columbia.

Equity

The amount of equity in the home. *Equity* is defined as the value of a property minus any outstanding loans. In most cases, the senior homeowner owns the property free and clear. If there is an outstanding mortgage loan balance still in place, it must be paid off at the time of closing. An advance may be made from the reverse mortgage loan to make this payment.

Age

This refers to the age of the borrowers, not the property. All borrowers on a reverse mortgage must be at least 62. There is no upper limit.

Interest Rate

Interest is the amount charged by the lender for the use of the principal and is generally charged in arrears (for the previous month). All interest charges on a reverse mortgage are calculated monthly and added to the principal amount. At the time the reverse mortgage loan is paid off, the principal, accrued interest, and any other charges will be included in the total amount due.

The interest rate to be charged on the FHA HECM is established weekly. Private lenders will charge market interest rate. More than 90 percent of all reverse mortgages made to date are FHA-insured home equity conversion mortgages. The HECM allows for either an annually adjusting rate, or a monthly adjusting rate. Some lenders offer both options, but some may only offer one or the other. The rates for the HECM are tied to U.S. security rates and the adjustment period remains the same once the loan has closed. Certain safeguards are built into the loans that provide limits on how much the interest rate may be increased. The annually adjusting rate may not increase more than 5 percent over the life of the loan, and no more than 2 percent in any year. The monthly adjusting rate may not increase by more than 10 percent over the life of the loan, but there is no limit to the amount the rate can change at monthly adjustments, although it must not exceed the 10 percent cap. The rate is adjusted up or down at either the annual or monthly adjustment period according to the current one-year treasury security at that time.

An initial rate of 7% may not increase beyond 9% in the first year on an annually adjusted basis (7 + 2 = 9). It may never increase beyond 12% over the life of the loan (7 + 5 = 12). A monthly adjusted rate starting at 7% may not increase beyond 17% over the life of the loan but there is no limit to the amount it may increase each month, although it may not exceed 17% (7 + 10 = 17).

The Home Keeper® mortgage is based on monthly adjustable rate interest. The rate is based on the current weekly average of the one-month Certificate of Deposit Index (CD Index) plus a margin determined by Fannie Mae. The CD Index may go up or down. The margin will remain the same. As of July 2002, the Fannie Mae margin for an annually adjusted rate was 2.1 percent; for monthly adjusted rates the margin is 1.5 percent. The rate may not increase by more than 12 percent over the life of the loan. There is no limit on the monthly increases as long as the 12 percent cap is not exceeded.

An initial rate of 7% may never increase beyond 19% over the life of the loan but may increase to any percent less than 19 in the next month, depending on the upward or downward movement of the CD index (7 + 12 = 19).

Interest rates may go either up or down depending on the index on which they are based. A change in the interest rate does not ever affect the amount or number of monthly payments that have been established in the reverse mortgage. The change in interest rate affects only the total loan balance. A higher rate of interest obviously increases the loan balance more than a lower rate of interest.

Based on an interest rate of 7 percent, the following chart shows an *approximation* of the amount available on a reverse mortgage. These amounts will be lower as interest rates go up, higher as interest rates go down.

Financing of closing costs, mortgage insurance premiums, and servicing fees are all variables that will affect the amount available. Adjustments to actual closing figures also must be made to compensate for variables such as a birthday falling between the date of application and the closing of the reverse mortgage loan. This could result in more funding being available if the borrower should move into a

HOME VALUE	AGE	LOAN AMOUNT AVAILABLE	
$ 100,000	65	$ 38,423	(38.4%)
	75	$ 50,815	(50.8%)
	85	$ 64,544	(64.5%)

Source: Home Made Money, AARP 1997

different age bracket. Any type of projections must always be considered as rough approximations, however; only after all factors have been taken into consideration can the lender provide an exact amount available for the borrower.

■ The Reverse Mortgage Calculator

The National Reverse Mortgage Lenders Association (NRMLA) is a nonprofit organization dedicated to providing valuable information for seniors who are considering employing the reverse mortgage in their plans to obtain or retain financial independence. NRMLA maintains a calculator for determining "how much you can get" on their Web site (*www.reversemortgage.org*). There is no charge to access this site. For someone who may not have a computer at home, the Web site can be accessed through computers at libraries, schools, or the homes of family members or friends. (There may be a nominal charge if information is to be printed out at libraries or schools.)

Because many seniors do not have access to a computer, this presents another opportunity for a real estate professional to assist them in obtaining this information. The real estate agent could also provide the senior homeowner an approximate figure to use for the value of the property.

There are four questions to be answered as shown in this hypothetical example:

When were you born?   **5/30/1936**

When was your spouse or other co-owner born?   **9/17/1935**

How much is your house worth? (best guess)   **$150,000**

Your Zip Code   **80016**

To Calculate: Click Once

Based on the above example, the senior homeowners could receive:

1. a single lump sum advance of **$71,572; OR**

2. a line-of-credit account of **$71,572** that grows larger each year if no draws are made; **OR**

3. a monthly loan advance for **$449** for as long as the seniors remained in the home; **OR**

4. any combination of lump sum at closing plus a line-of-credit account, or monthly advance.

Variables

The numbers that appear on the Reverse Mortgage Calculator will vary when different zip codes are used. This is due to the FHA maximum loan amount available, which is based on housing costs by specific areas. The automated results still provide an approximate idea of how much cash will be available through the reverse mortgage loan. Actual amounts will also depend on other conditions that may prevail at time of closing, such as reimbursement from the mortgage lender for home appraisal. At the time of application, the mortgage lender will require a check to cover the cost of an appraisal and a credit report. When the loan closes, all costs, including reimbursement for the appraisal and credit report, can be rolled into the mortgage loan, leaving the homeowner's finances intact; in other words, no money out-of-pocket.

The Reverse Mortgage Calculator is a simple tool that may help senior homeowners consider the possibilities that are open to them. Because the variables are so great from one location to another and the percentage of the value that may be allowed for the total loan amount varies greatly depending on current interest rates, it should be thought of as presenting the broad picture only, never a definitive statement of fact.

■ Summary

In this chapter the importance of seeking reverse mortgage borrower counseling is stressed. No less important is the process of selecting a reverse mortgage lender. The reverse mortgage loan is not difficult but it is quite different from the usual homebuyer mortgage loan that can be originated by any lender anywhere. Because of the unique aspects of the reverse mortgage loan, senior homeowners need to be assured that they are working with a lender who understands both the technicalities of the loan itself and the particular needs of the senior borrowers.

Using the Mortgage Calculator provided by the NRMLA on their Web site can provide an estimated amount of lump sum advance, credit line, or monthly payments that may be obtained. The amount available will vary according to the location and market value of the property and the age of the borrowers—the older the seniors, the higher the percentage of their the home value available to them on a reverse mortgage.

In effect, all of the costs of initiating a reverse mortgage loan can be included in the loan itself, requiring no monies out-of-pocket from the senior borrowers. Fees such as those charged for appraisal and credit checks that are charged at the time of application will be reimbursed to the borrowers at settlement.

■ Chapter 3 Review Questions

1. Jack is considering taking out a reverse mortgage. His first step should be to
   a. call a REALTOR® to look at properties for sale.
   b. call a mortgage lender to apply for a loan.
   c. locate a HUD-approved reverse mortgage housing counselor.
   d. check with his heirs to see if they have any objection.

2. A counseling session with a HUD-approved housing counselor should last
   a. two hours.
   b. two hours each for two sessions.
   c. four hours.
   d. four hours each for two sessions.

3. The most important thing to consider in selecting a reverse mortgage lender for a home equity conversion mortgage is to
   a. shop around for the one with the lowest interest rate.
   b. choose a lender with experience in reverse mortgage loans.
   c. look for a lender who quotes the lowest closing costs.
   d. seek out the lender who will discount the origination fee.

4. The amount of total funds available for a reverse mortgage would only increase when using the
   a. tenure plan.
   b. term plan.
   c. line-of-credit plan.
   d. lump sum plan.

5. The amount of available credit for a home equity conversion mortgage will be limited by the
   a. current Fannie Mae loan limit.
   b. current FHA loan limit for that geographic area.
   c. financial assets of the borrowers.
   d. decision of the lender.

6. The amount available for a Home Keeper® reverse mortgage will be limited by the
   a. current Fannie Mae loan limit.
   b. current FHA loan limit for that geographic area.
   c. financial assets of the borrowers.
   d. decision of the lender.

7. Which of the following statements with regard to interest paid on a reverse mortgage loan is NOT true?
   a. Interest is what the lender charges for the use of the principal funds.
   b. Interest accrued on March 1 is usually for the previous month.
   c. Interest on a HECM is calculated weekly and must be paid each month.
   d. Interest is added to the principal balance and paid when the reverse mortgage is terminated.

8. Although an approximation of the amount that will be available on a reverse mortgage can be estimated, the final amount will depend on all of the following EXCEPT
   a. how the funds are to be used by the borrower.
   b. closing costs that are included with the loan.
   c. payoff of existing mortgage or other bills.
   d. changes in the interest rate.

9. If the interest rate on an annually adjusted home equity conversion mortgage starts at 8%, the maximum rate over the life of the loan will be limited to
   a. 10%.
   b. 13%.
   c. 18%.
   d. 20%.

10. Seniors obtaining a reverse mortgage loan should expect to pay out-of-pocket for
    a. the origination fee.
    b. the servicing fee.
    c. the credit report and appraisal.
    d. nothing.

Reverse Mortgage Expenses, Fees, and Closing Costs

learning objectives

After completing this chapter, you will be able to:

- discuss the schedule involved in obtaining a reverse mortgage;

- list the categories of costs for a reverse mortgage loan;

- give an example of anticipated closing costs on a reverse mortgage loan; and

- describe expected loan costs after closing.

■ Key Terms

Closing Costs

Escrow Funds

Federal Income Tax

Home Inspection

Homeowner Insurance

Mortgage Insurance (MIP or PMI)

Periodic Statements

Points

Recording Fees

Settlement

Student Loan

Survey

Title Insurance

Total Annual Loan Cost (TALC)

Seniors need a plan tailored to provide answers to economic needs. These needs are neither distant nor probabilities of the future—they exist today. The U.S. Labor Department has stated that about six in ten workers reach retirement age without benefit of a regular pension. This leaves them largely dependent on Social Security, which on average covers two-thirds of an older middle-class person's needs. The reverse mortgage can provide a path to bridging this gap; but it will take time and will be costly.

Timing when attempting to obtain a reverse mortgage loan is generally not as important to seniors as it is to people purchasing a home, where certain deadlines for moving are more critical. Seniors are already in their homes and are not planning to move anywhere. In the exceptional case where timing is important, this should be considered and openly discussed with the mortgage lender.

The reverse mortgage loan will usually take four to six weeks from the time of loan application to the date of closing. This is longer than the time needed to obtain a regular mortgage loan to purchase property.

■ Closing Costs for a Reverse Mortgage Loan

What Is It Going To Cost?

Closing costs are not cheap; in fact, the grand total may create a mild shock for the prospective borrower. A review of typical charges that will be necessary to close on a reverse mortgage loan should be explained to the borrowers well in advance of closing. As it usually will have been a number of years since the homeowners closed on their last "forward" mortgage, it may help to recall the amount that was charged for such items as lender origination fees and/or points on that earlier loan.

Moreover, recalling the cost of items such as an appraisal, credit report, survey, possibly a **home inspection,** and a **mortgage insurance** premium (**MIP** on an FHA loan) or private mortgage insurance (**PMI** on a conventional loan with less than 20 percent down payment), will remind the homeowners of the expenses accompanying the process.

If a property was purchased during a slow market time, the builder or the seller may have paid some or all of the closing costs to provide strong incentives to close the transaction. With a reverse mortgage there is no one to make offers of that type. Closing costs are unavoidable and there is no one to pay them except those obtaining the loan. Every dollar of closing costs is allocated to paying someone or some organization for services currently rendered or to be performed in the future. Generally, these closing costs can be reimbursed to the borrower during the settlement on the loan.

Total Annual Loan Cost (TALC)

Federal law requires that lenders disclose the **Total Annual Loan Cost (TALC)** for every reverse mortgage. As the TALC combines all of the loan's costs into one total, it is useful in comparing the cost of one reverse mortgage with another.

Taking a close look at the bottom line TALC figure will show that the longer seniors remain in the home, the less expensive the loan will be. The upfront costs of the loan (origination fee, closing costs, and insurance premium) represent a large part of the total amount paid at closing. When these costs are spread out over a short period of time the reverse mortgage loan becomes very expensive. As the loan balance grows over a number of years, the upfront costs are spread out over a longer period of time. In fact, if the loan's balance catches up to the home's value, the true cost of the loan will continue to decrease at an even higher rate. The longer the homeowners remain in the home, the less expensive the reverse mortgage loan will turn out to be.

Closing costs of $3,000 dollars on a total loan amount of $60,000 that only lasts for five years would represent a cost of 1% per year. ($3,000 divided by $60,000 = 5% divided by five years.

If the reverse mortgage stayed in place for 20 years the cost would be reduced to almost nothing (5% divided by 20 years = 0.25%).

Home Equity Conversion Mortgage

The itemized costs for the FHA Home Equity Conversion Mortgage (HECM) are generally higher than those charged for a typical forward mortgage or home equity loan. The benefits provided by the HECM, as reiterated below, more than offset the difference in costs.

- No monthly payments are required.
- The open-ended monthly cash advance continues as long as the seniors remain in the home.
- No repayment of the loan is required as long as the seniors remain in the home.
- In the case of a line-of-credit reverse mortgage, the amount available is guaranteed to increase until the total sum has been used.
- The total debt may not exceed the value of the home, no matter how long the seniors live, and no matter what changes may occur in the value of the home.

Closing costs for a HECM in most cases will be less than those charged for a proprietary (private lender) reverse mortgage. The following are itemized costs that can be expected with a HECM loan.

Application Fee   The application fee covers the cost of the property appraisal and a credit check. The appraisal is to determine the value of the home; the credit check provides a snapshot of the prospective borrowers' credit history. Of particular interest is whether there are any outstanding loans for money received from the federal government. The application fee is charged at the time of loan application and usually represents the only amount of cash that must be paid out-of-pocket by the borrowers. It may, however, be included in the loan package; if so, the amount will be reimbursed to the borrower at closing.

Origination Fee   The origination fee is paid to the lender for preparing the paperwork and processing the loan. New origination fees for reverse mortgages are now capped at the greater of $2,000 or 2 percent of the value of the home, not to exceed the FHA allowable maximum area loan amount. The origination fee may vary from one lender to another.

Closing Costs   The closing, also referred to as **settlement,** is the day on which the mortgage begins. Closing is handled differently in different parts of the country but it generally involves a meeting of the parties involved where all legal documents are signed to finalize the transaction. Several third parties provide services required for closing. These services include, but are not limited to, a search of title and provision of **title insurance,** a **survey** of the property, a **home inspection** if required, **recording fees** to the county and state, and property taxes. Closing costs will vary according to the value of the home as some of the fees are calculated on a percentage basis, but generally third-party closing costs will not vary much from one lender to another.

Mortgage Insurance Premium A mortgage insurance premium is charged on all HECM loans. This cost consists of two separate parts and may be rolled into the loan balance. The two parts of the premium are:

1. a one-time charge of 2 percent of the home's value or 2 percent of the FHA local area loan limit, whichever is less. This charge can be financed as part of the loan; and

2. 0.5 percent of the loan balance per year, an annual premium divided by 12 and charged monthly. This charge is added to the loan balance.

This mortgage insurance premium guarantees that the monthly advances will continue and that no repayment of the loan must be made as long as the seniors live in the home. It further guarantees that regardless of any change in value of the property, the total loan balance due can never exceed the maximum claim amount that is determined at the origination of the loan. No deficit created by a drop in value of the home will be charged to the senior homeowners, their estate, or their heirs.

Servicing Fee The amount charged for servicing the loan includes many different services. As this can vary greatly between lenders, it is important to verify, prior to closing, exactly how much will be charged for any of the following:

- Generating loan advances or any changes requested
- Transferring insurance premiums to FHA
- Sending account statements
- Paying property taxes and insurance from the loan if requested
- Monitoring the borrowers' compliance with the obligations of the loan agreement

FHA places a limit of $30 per month for servicing fees if the loan has an annual adjustable interest rate, and $35 if the interest rate is adjusted monthly. If this fee is to be financed as part of the loan, the lender must set a specific dollar amount to be added to the loan balance each month.

Paying separately for a servicing fee will sound strange to most senior borrowers. In the traditional forward mortgage this fee is calculated into the interest rate charged.

Closing Cost Example

Based on a market value of $150,000 the following closing costs would be expected. The various charges may vary slightly depending on the geographic location of the property. All of the charges will appear on the HUD-1 Settlement Statement that is required by law.

1. **$3,000 Mortgage Loan Origination Fee**
   This is the money that makes it possible for the mortgage lender to rent an office; cover office expenses; meet payroll for assistants, such as computer operators and mortgage loan counselors; and, it is hoped, show a fair profit for all of the time and energy expended.

   Commonly referred to as **"points,"** under congressional mandates approved in 2001, new loan origination fees for reverse mortgages are now capped at the greater of $2,000 or 2 percent of the value of the home but not to exceed the FHA allowable maximum area loan amount.

2. **$3,000 Mortgage Insurance Premium (MIP)**

   This cost represents payment to the FHA Mortgage Insurance Fund that guarantees payment to each reverse mortgage participant as long as he or she lives in the home.

   In the event of the inability or unwillingness of a mortgage company to make the agreed-upon payments, FHA, with the full faith and credit of the U.S. government, steps in and makes all payments to the senior homeowner as agreed.

   If the payout should exceed the value of the home, the checks will continue as long as the seniors remain in the home. There is never a charge back to their estate for excess payouts to the senior homeowner or surviving spouse.

3. **$350 Home Appraisal Fee**

   The mortgage lender will order an appraisal of the home at the time of application for the reverse mortgage. The lender will require a check or credit card from the prospective borrowers at the time of application. Alternatively, the lender may have an arrangement in place whereby the senior pays an independent FHA-approved appraiser directly. The reason for advance payment is to make sure there is money on hand to pay the appraiser for the service performed in case the prospective borrower decides not to proceed with the loan. The amount can be repaid to the borrower at closing by having the lender roll the cost into the mortgage loan.

4. **$300 Home Inspection**

   A home inspection may be necessary if the home needs repairs or desirable updating. Costly repairs such as a new heating system can be covered by reserves set aside for that particular purpose and will be paid for at closing from the proceeds of the reverse mortgage loan.

5. **$600 Title Insurance Coverage**

   Insurance to guarantee marketable title, free and clear of all liens, encumbrances, encroachments, and other claims, whether valid or not, shown against the property must be obtained. Wrap-around policies covering the borrower, the mortgage lender, and FHA must be purchased. This is a one-time charge.

6. **$75 Credit Report**

   A credit report is required even though there are no financial requirements for qualifying other than having the home free and clear of debt (or nearly paid off).

   The reason for the credit report is to make sure that there are no outstanding **federal income taxes,** unpaid **student loans,** or other items that could take priority over the new first note and trust deed or mortgage. If there are any such liens they will have to be paid off or be released if they have already been paid or if they are in error. The reverse mortgage loan counselor can provide guidance in having these items satisfied. The lender will require payment for the credit check at time of application but this can be reimbursed at time of closing by rolling the cost into the mortgage loan.

7. **$100 Recording and Miscellaneous Fees**

   Certain documents have to be recorded with the county or parish clerk and recorder; for example, the deed of trust or mortgage and releases of prior instruments of debt.

8. **Survey Fee**

   A new survey of the land and home may be required, particularly if other homes were built adjacent to the property following the original purchase. It may be helpful to provide a copy of the original survey to the reverse mortgage loan counselor at the time of application as it could be determined that a new survey will not be necessary.

Total Sample Closing Cost = $7,425

Frequently Asked Questions about Closing Costs

Who Pays Closing Costs?   In the above example, the closing costs estimate represents 4.95% of the value of the home. ($150,000 x 4.95 = $7,425). Although there are always ways to justify the cost of obtaining money to accomplish the things one wants to do in life, it will ultimately depend on each individual's perception of value received to satisfy their wants and needs.

Most buyers pay closing costs upon purchasing a home as there does not appear to be any logical reason for their not paying them. As seen above, each item of expense is disbursed to individuals and organizations that provide specific service. In the case of a home purchase, sellers or builders may pay some or all of these closing costs as an inducement to make the sale. With the reverse mortgage there is no one else to look to. The senior homeowners must accept paying their own closing costs, remembering that these costs can be financed into the total loan package.

Where Does Closing Occur?   The reverse mortgage lender who took the loan application in the seniors' home can probably offer the same level of service for closing the transaction. It is often possible to conduct the entire process in the comfort of the homeowner's home. In other cases, the lenders may prefer to close the reverse mortgage loan at a local title insurance and escrow office.

■ Costs after Closing

There is little difference between costs associated with a reverse mortgage and that which all homeowners experience while making payments on a forward mortgage. The principal difference is the manner in which interest is handled. On a forward mortgage the cost of interest is paid monthly as part of the regular payment. Taxes and insurance are commonly bundled into the total monthly payment and are paid from escrow funds set up by the mortgage lender.

No type of reverse mortgage requires payments of any kind until the senior homeowners either decide to sell or move out of their home for more than 12 months. The ongoing cost for interest is added to a running balance each month and paid in full when the loan is paid off. The FHA Mortgage Insurance Premium is handled the same way. Additionally, senior homeowners are charged a monthly service fee. This covers the cost of the mortgage lender to administer the account. Real estate taxes and **homeowners insurance** will continue to be paid by the senior homeowners unless special arrangements are made for them to be paid by the lender.

Monthly Costs on the Reverse Mortgage Loan

In addition to the principal loan balance that will increase as each payment is made to the homeowner, other charges will be added or change each month. These include the rate of interest, the mortgage insurance premium, and the service fee.

Adjustable Rate Interest   The rate of interest is adjusted each month based upon a selected weekly average yield of U.S. Treasury securities, plus an agreed-upon margin of return. In effect, this means that the interest rate floats with the market. It can go up or it can go down. It is this feature plus the FHA insurance that makes the reverse mortgage loan attractive to investors.

A steady stream of investors willing to purchase reverse mortgage loans is necessary to keep the supply of funds available for reverse mortgage loans at an adequate level to ensure that every senior who qualifies and wishes to obtain such a loan will be able to do so. Fannie Mae purchases reverse mortgage loans (HECMs) and packages them as mortgage-backed securities. Investors purchase these securities, which provide Fannie Mae with more funds with which to purchase more HECMs from local lenders.

Also attractive to investors are the annually adjusted rate mortgages that may be offered instead of the monthly-adjusted rate mortgages. Both have annual and maximum rate caps, which means they can only be increased up to those stated limits. The early years of the 21st century have seen dramatic downward interest adjustments from highs of 9 percent to lows of less than 4 percent for adjustable rate mortgages.

ARM Monthly Statement   Anyone who has a monthly adjustable rate mortgage will receive a monthly statement giving the current status of the interest rate. It will look something like this:

Interest Rate Change Notice

In accordance with the terms of your Adjustable Rate Note, this is your notification that effective _____ (month) _____ (year), the interest rate on your loan will change from _____ to _____. The initial interest rate of your mortgage was _____, which may not be increased beyond _____ during the life of the mortgage.

Mortgage Insurance Premium (MIP)   There is an ongoing charge for covering the risk of FHA in insuring the mortgage pool. In case of a shortfall, FHA covers the agreement in full, no matter how much is paid out, without recourse to the estate of the senior homeowner. There is never a recovery from an individual senior or benefactors of their estate.

Monthly premium = 0.5% per year divided by 12		
$	150,000	FHA coverage
x	0.05	MIP charge
$	750	Annual charge (divided by 12)
$	62.50	**Monthly mortgage insurance premium**

Service Fee   The mortgage lender will impose a fee for servicing the mortgage loan. The fee varies, ranging from $25 to $35 per month. The monthly cost will be added to the principal balance, as shown in the example below:

$	60,000	Lump sum reverse mortgage (distributed to senior homeowner)
+	200	Interest for January ($60,000 @ 4% per year = $2400 divided by 12 = $200)
+	62	MIP January charge
+	30	Service fee for January
$	**60,292**	**Current outstanding balance total**

All costs are added to the principal balance each month. No money is due to be paid by the senior homeowner until the reverse mortgage loan is paid off. The reverse mortgage loan may be paid off at any time, without penalty.

If the homeowners had elected to take a tenure plan or term plan the principal would start at 0 and the monthly payout would be added to the sum to make a new principal balance each month.

$	450.00	January payout on tenure plan
+	1.50	Interest for January ($450 x 4% = $18/12 = $1.50)
+	62.00	MIP January charge
+	30.00	January service fee
$	**543.50**	**Current outstanding balance total**

Periodic Status Statements

The lender sends out **periodic status statements** every three months with a complete summarization of the activity as described in the above examples. The statements show the beginning balance, the amount added for interest, the amount charged for mortgage insurance premium, the service fee paid, and the amount of principal disbursement, if any.

Both the tenure and the term plans have a regular principal disbursement each month as agreed upon in the terms of the reverse mortgage. With a lump sum plan there is only one principal disbursement at closing. With a line-of-credit plan, principal disbursements are shown only as funds are drawn down.

■ Additional Costs

Escrow for Homeowner's Insurance

The mortgage lender can also escrow premiums **(escrow funds)** for homeowner's insurance. With a tenure or term plan, the lender deducts from the monthly check one-twelfth of the annual cost and pays the insurance company once each year. If the lender is not making this payment, the homeowner must be sure to keep current on the insurance company payments. As the lender is listed as co-insured, the lender will be notified by the insurance company if the premiums are not paid.

Maintenance and Repairs

Although most people are not aware of this, any mortgage can be declared in default if the borrower fails to maintain the property in good condition or neglects to make repairs as needed. Senior homeowners have usually lived in their present home for many years and are well aware of the importance of regular maintenance.

A major catastrophe such as a broken water main or a failed septic field could create a tremendous financial problem. Rather than panic, the holders of a reverse mortgage should immediately contact the mortgage lender. The lender will do everything possible to restore the property—and the homeowners' life—back to normal.

■ Summary

The issue of closing costs may often provoke apprehension and a sense of distrust from a senior homeowner considering a reverse mortgage. It is very important that all aspects of each of the closing costs involved when obtaining a reverse mortgage be explained in detail. It may also be necessary to explain the rationale for the homeowner's having to absorb these costs into the reverse mortgage loan.

The initial costs will be similar for each of the four different reverse mortgage plans but the ongoing costs may vary depending on whether it is a tenure, term, line of credit, or lump sum type of mortgage. In any case, the lender will provide a monthly statement showing each of the charges for that particular month and for the current principal loan balance.

The real estate professional can play an important role in assuaging fears by reviewing the list of closing costs, reassuring the senior homeowner that these costs are normal and to be expected. Because of the special circumstances involved financing a reverse mortgage, there is a need for slow and careful discussion of all elements. A comparison to a typical HUD-1 Settlement Sheet for a conventional forward mortgage may be helpful in establishing which costs are expected on any type of mortgage and which ones pertain only to a reverse mortgage.

■ Chapter 4 Review Questions

1. The time from application to closing on a reverse mortgage is generally
   a. two weeks.
   b. four weeks.
   c. four to six weeks.
   d. six to eight weeks.

2. Which of the following statements with regard to closing costs on a reverse mortgage is true?
   a. The senior borrowers will not have to pay closing costs.
   b. The senior borrowers will have to pay only part of the closing costs.
   c. The senior borrowers will have to pay all of the closing costs in cash at the time of settlement.
   d. The senior borrowers will have to pay all of the closing costs but the costs can be rolled into the loan.

3. All of the following are costs that could be charged at closing EXCEPT
   a. appraisal and credit report.
   b. survey.
   c. origination fee.
   d. maintenance reserve.

4. All of the following insurance charges could be included in closing costs EXCEPT
   a. FHA MIP.
   b. conventional PMI.
   c. homeowner's insurance.
   d. borrower's life insurance.

5. The Smiths have just taken out a reverse mortgage with total loan costs of $7,500. Which of the following statements is true?
   a. If they stay in the property for 20 years, the reverse mortgage will have been less expensive.
   b. If they leave the property after 5 years, the reverse mortgage will have been more expensive.
   c. The total loan costs are the same so the expense of the loan will not vary.
   d. The total loan costs have no bearing on the expense of the loan.

6. The total loan costs for the FHA HECM are generally
   a. higher than for a typical forward mortgage, and higher than for a proprietary reverse mortgage.
   b. lower than for a typical forward mortgage, and higher than for a proprietary reverse mortgage.
   c. higher than for a typical forward mortgage, but lower than for a proprietary reverse mortgage.
   d. lower than for a typical forward mortgage, but higher than for a proprietary reverse mortgage.

7. Which of the following benefits provided by the HECM could be the most important to aging seniors and their heirs?
   a. No monthly payments.
   b. Monthly advances continue as long as the seniors remain in the home.
   c. No repayment is required until the reverse mortgage is terminated.
   d. The total debt may not exceed the value of the home, no matter how long the seniors live.

8. A credit check is required on a reverse mortgage loan application to

   a. determine the applicant's credit score.

   b. make sure the senior homeowners do not have too many credit cards.

   c. identify any outstanding student or other government loans.

   d. verify history for making timely mortgage payments.

9. Title insurance is required on a reverse mortgage loan for all of the following reasons EXCEPT

   a. to insure that there are no previous claims to title to the property.

   b. to protect the lender from future claims against the property.

   c. to protect the borrower(s) from future claims against the property.

   d. to pay for preparation of the deed granting title to the property.

10. Certain costs that should be anticipated after closing on a reverse mortgage loan include all of the following EXCEPT

    a. adjustable rate interest charged on the principal balance.

    b. FHA 0.05% mortgage insurance premium on a HECM loan.

    c. lender fee for servicing the loan.

    d. title insurance monthly premiums.

Tax Benefits and Treatments: Annuity Issues and Rebuilding an Estate

learning objectives

After completing this chapter, you will be able to:

- explain how tax deductions apply to reverse mortgage loans;

- discuss the option of adding an annuity with a reverse mortgage;

- describe the way a senior may rebuild his or her estate; and

- illustrate the benefit of returning to the workplace.

■ Key Terms

Annuity	Tax Reporting Service	Total Finance Charges
Homeowner's Property Tax		

Although the real estate professional must always be on guard not to appear to be giving legal or tax advice, it is helpful to have a general knowledge of how some aspects of both tax and accounting issues are affected by a reverse mortgage. More detailed information can be found at *www.irs.gov.*

■ Tax Benefits and Treatments

The most substantial benefit of homeownership versus renting is that all interest paid on a mortgage loan is deductible. This often results in a new homeowner being able to purchase a home with no additional out-of-pocket expense than that incurred when renting. Senior homeowners were used to having this benefit for many years as they gradually paid off their home mortgage. It is important that senior homeowners now entering into a reverse mortgage become aware of how the interest deduction will be handled on their reverse mortgage loan.

Allowable Tax Deductions

Total Finance Charges   The reverse mortgage lender provides a statement at year-end that lists the amount of **total finance charges** accrued to date. The amount of interest accrued will be listed as well as the amount of FHA or private mortgage insurance premiums that have been charged during the past year. The combination of the two equals the total finance charges accrued from the beginning of the mortgage loan to the end of the year. This can be an important document for federal income tax purposes at the time when the property is sold.

Interest   The interest on a reverse mortgage is not deductible on a current year basis for federal income tax purposes. The total finance charges accrue each year and are added to the principal sum owed to the mortgage lender. These charges are not paid until the mortgage loan is paid off. At that time, the total accrued amount of interest paid is deductible for federal income tax filing for that year. The Internal Revenue Service (IRS) has a long-standing rule that prohibits the deduction of interest for home mortgages until the sum claimed is actually paid. This deduction may only be taken if the seniors are filing an itemized, rather than a standard, income tax return. In many cases the seniors will not have an income flow sufficiently large for the deduction to be of any benefit.

Homeowner's Property Tax   Under the tenure or term plan reverse mortgages, the seniors can either pay the **homeowner's property taxes** as they become due or they may request that their mortgage lender escrow a sum equal to one-twelfth of the annual taxes each month. This amount will be subtracted from the monthly check. The lender will then pay the tax bill when it is due. Arrangement for the payment of property taxes by the mortgage lender can also be done under the credit-line or lump sum reverse mortgages. This arrangement should be made with the lender at the time of loan application.

Property taxes as paid by senior homeowners are deductible on an annual basis, if itemized returns are filed.

Importance of Tax Payments   Mortgage lenders must be sure that the taxes due on the property are paid in a timely manner. If the taxes are not paid within the deadlines set up by the taxing authority, the property is subject to a tax sale. The right to claim title to the home is sold, subject to certain conditions, to the highest bidder. Buyers of tax certificates will usually bid the amount of the delinquent taxes with premiums being paid for particularly attractive parcels.

The difficulties a tax sale would cause are staggering. Rather than let the property go to auction, the lender would pay delinquent taxes plus accrued charges for interest and charge the total back to the reverse mortgage account. In the case of a lump sum reverse mortgage, the tax liability could cause the lender to extend more funds than would be prudent. If no more funds were available in the account the lender would most likely order a new appraisal and issue a notice of repayment based on the new numbers.

Tax Reporting Service   To avoid any potential problem with nonpayment of taxes, the mortgage lender will usually subscribe to a **tax reporting service.** This service will keep them not only informed, but assured that the property taxes are paid each year. If the lender is escrowing for property taxes each month, the senior borrower might be exempt from this charge. The cost of the service is reasonable; if charged, it will show up as a continuing charge to the account. There will be no money out-of-pocket as the charge will be paid and added to the total principal mortgage each year.

Property Tax and Special Assessment Deductibility   Similar to the way the federal tax deduction for interest is handled, home property taxes and special assessment taxes paid each year are deductible for income tax purposes, but only if an itemized return is filed.

Deferred Payment Program   If the senior homeowners are participating in a deferred tax payment program where the state pays the tax for the homeowner, the federal deduction cannot be taken until all back taxes due are paid. At that time, all accrued taxes paid back to the state are deductible against income for the year in which they were actually paid. Again, this applies only if an itemized tax return is filed.

Although tax benefits may not be a significant issue for senior homeowners as it is likely that they are now in a lower income tax bracket, it is still something to be considered. It is especially important that the senior homeowner understands the implications of the reverse mortgage with regard to the payment of mortgage loan interest and home property and special assessments taxes.

No deductions may be applied to federal income tax until the amounts are actually paid. This means that accrued interest on the loan and any property taxes paid by the lender and then added to the principal amount of the reverse mortgage loan may not be used as a deductible item until the property is sold and the reverse mortgage loan is paid off. This does not normally occur until the reverse mortgage borrowers are either deceased or have chosen to leave the property, selling the home to repay the reverse mortgage loan.

Compiling information on both tax benefits and tax credits that are available in a given market area provides an opportunity for the local REALTOR® or other real estate professional to offer special service to their senior clients. Tax issues specific to an individual should, of course, be handled by a professional who specializes in that subject, but provision of general information of interest or benefit to clients is always appropriate for the real estate professional.

■ Adding an Annuity

An option to be considered with a reverse mortgage is to use the money derived from the reverse mortgage to purchase an **annuity.** Annuities also provide a monthly advance but the amount may not be as secure as that received through the Home Equity Conversion Mortgage (HECM). A careful study should be made before entering into any annuity program in connection with the reverse mortgage.

Senior homeowners who have just obtained the HECM are sometimes strongly encouraged by an insurance agent to purchase an annuity with the proceeds from the reverse mortgage loan. There is absolutely no obligation to use the funds in this way. The HECM provides for monthly advances for as long as the seniors remain in the home. An annuity may also promise monthly advances but it may be tied to the stock market or other investments with no guarantee of the amount of monthly payment.

Adding an annuity to the HECM will result in higher costs than with the HECM alone. There may also be tax consequences on funds received through an annuity. One additional problem for seniors who are receiving supplemental security income (SSI) or Medicaid is that annuity advances may jeopardize the benefits received from these programs. Further information on how to make a side-by-side comparison of the HECM plus annuity with the HECM alone can be found on the AARP Web site, *www.aarp.org*.

■ Rebuilding an Estate

One of the big concerns of many seniors about taking out a reverse mortgage is the fear of diminishing the value of the their estate. This is a valid consideration and should be openly discussed with all members of the family who will be affected.

The general consensus of people who actually have a reverse mortgage is that the financial independence it creates for the seniors involved is worth the decrease in the eventual estate. The amount of decrease is more than offset by relieving the family members involved from the practical necessity of providing adequate funding for the seniors' living expenses during the extended period of their lives.

Changing Attitudes

In the decades of the 1930s and 1940s U.S. home ownership was confined to a small number of people. Approximately 30 percent of families owned their own homes and building an estate was scaled to modest expectations. Even so, a strong ethic prevailed in all societies that leaving an estate, however modest, was a personal mark of pride and achievement.

Senior homeowners today are the children of that generation and most have a concern about touching any of the assets of the expanded value of their estates. With more than 67 percent of all U.S. citizens now owning homes with astronomically increased value, this is a treasure chest they plan to pass on to their children or other heirs. Nonetheless, the ebb and flow of life causes a reexamination of personal finances in times of crises, need, or the wish to execute the demands of one's desires.

A Return to the Workplace

Acknowledging that any reverse mortgage may draw down the total asset value of their estate, what can senior homeowners do to rebuild its value during their lifetime? It may be useful to think about rebuilding, as personal needs decrease with the passage of time. Absent the ill fortune of poor health, many seniors reverse their income stream after a somewhat dormant period of retirement by returning to the workplace.

A good case in point was the Year 2000 U.S. census. The Census Bureau hired more than 500,000 people temporarily to help in their yearlong process of counting all of the people in the United States. Tens of thousands were seniors who wanted something to do and desired some extra income. All of them had pensions or Social Security and their incomes were for the most part adequate to sustain their needs. Some had reverse mortgages. After working for close to a year many of these seniors had accumulated savings of around $10,000.

With no immediate needs for the extra income, suppose such a person decided to pay down a reverse mortgage.

$	12,000	Current reverse mortgage balance
×	0.07	Current interest rate
$	**3,500**	**Annual interest cost**
$	50,000	Current reverse mortgage balance
−	10,000	Repayment
$	**40,000**	**New reverse mortgage balance**
$	40,000	New reverse mortgage balance
×	0.07	Annual interest rate
$	**2,800**	**Annual interest cost**
$	3,500	Annual interest cost @ $50,000
−	2,800	Annual interest cost @ $40,000
$	**700**	**Annual interest savings**

In addition to interest savings, there may be income tax benefits because annual interest accrued on a reverse mortgage is not deductible until paid. The $10,000 repaid in this example makes available for deduction from federal income tax all accrued interest on the $10,000 from the date of inception of the reverse mortgage to the date of payoff. This would apply only for senior homeowners who file itemized federal income tax returns. The deduction could easily offset any tax due to the extra income earned for the year.

A senior homeowner with a reverse mortgage of, say, $50,000 could work for about six years and completely pay off the principal plus interest due to the mortgage company, restoring the estate to full integrity.

Holding the Reverse Mortgage in Reserve

A safety net is built into the rebuilding of the estate. All money repaid to the mortgage company is automatically available for use by the senior homeowners through switching plans or starting a new plan if the need or desire to do so comes up in the future.

After retirement, many seniors discover a need to experience daily interaction with other people and reenter the work force on a full or part-time basis. If they have a reverse mortgage and are concerned about rebuilding their estates, a pay-down on the outstanding balance could provide an exciting inducement to justify the activity.

■ Summary

For most senior homeowners considering a reverse mortgage, the FHA Home Equity Conversion Mortgage (HECM) appears to be the best choice. Both the requirements and the benefits are established by FHA/HUD thereby giving the seniors the assurance that their reverse mortgage is backed by the full strength of the U.S. government. The one drawback to the HECM is that the actual loan is limited by the FHA loan limits that are set for each geographic area throughout the country. If the seniors' home exceeds the limits set for their particular area, they might do better to consider obtaining the reverse mortgage from one of the proprietary lenders. Generally, the proprietary reverse mortgage will cost more to obtain and service but the increased benefits might make it worthwhile.

Rebuilding an estate that has been depleted by a reverse mortgage may be very important to some seniors. Those persons now in the "older seniors" category (born before 1925) have been raised to "burn the mortgage" and leave an appreciable estate when they die. Providing for the heirs does not seem to be as important to the rising seniors—the baby boomers—but for the oldest of the senior homeowners this can be a very significant factor. Knowing that the reverse mortgage loan balance can be repaid in part or totally during their lifetimes may help senior homeowners make the decision to obtain a reverse mortgage to provide funds for immediate needs. Remembering that the repaid loan can always be reactivated in any of the four reverse mortgage plans assures the senior homeowners that their financial needs can be covered no matter what may occur in the future.

■ Chapter 5 Review Questions

1. Which of the following statements regarding the deductibility of interest on a reverse mortgage is not true?

    a. The lender will provide the homeowner with an annual statement listing total finance charges to date.

    b. The amount of interest plus mortgage insurance premiums are included in the total finance charges.

    c. The interest paid on a reverse mortgage is deductible in the year it is charged.

    d. The interest paid on a reverse mortgage is not deductible until the time the reverse mortgage is paid off.

2. Which of the following statements regarding the property taxes on a reverse mortgage is not true?

    a. The homeowner is still liable for annual property taxes.

    b. The homeowner must pay property taxes out-of-pocket each year.

    c. The lender may pay the taxes by escrowing a sum equal to 1/12 of the amount each month and deducting it from the monthly advance.

    d. Property taxes are deductible from income tax and may be claimed at the time the reverse mortgage loan is paid off.

3. To ensure that property taxes are paid in a timely fashion, the lender may

    a. require a cancelled check from the homeowner.

    b. check each month with the local taxing authority.

    c. subscribe to a tax reporting service.

    d. pay the tax and backcharge the homeowner.

4. All of the following are allowable as deductions from federal income tax at the time the reverse mortgage loan is paid off EXCEPT

    a. interest on the principal.

    b. property taxes.

    c. special assessment taxes.

    d. accrued monthly service fees.

5. Jack and Marie have been told that their state will allow them to defer payment for their property taxes until such time that their reverse mortgage is paid off. The federal deduction for property tax may be taken at this time as long as

    a. Jack and Marie have paid their state tax bill.

    b. Jack and Marie file an itemized tax return.

    c. Jack and Marie are considered to be in poverty level.

    d. Jack and Marie are registered voters.

6. Tax issues specific to individual homeowners should be handled by

    a. their REALTOR®.

    b. the lender.

    c. a tax professional.

    d. the closing agent.

7. Adding an annuity to a home equity conversion mortgage

    a. is mandatory with a HECM.

    b. costs the homeowner no extra money.

    c. has no impact on Medicaid.

    d. should be carefully researched before purchasing.

8. Which of the following statements is true regarding the effect of a reverse mortgage on a senior homeowner's estate?

    a. It is never possible to rebuild an estate once a reverse mortgage is taken out.

    b. There is absolutely no benefit to family members when seniors decide to take out a reverse mortgage.

    c. The fact the reverse mortgage will diminish the value of an estate should be discussed openly with members of the family who will be affected.

    d. There is never any possibility for the senior homeowner to pay off the reverse mortgage during his or her lifetime.

9. Homeownership in the United States today is slightly over
   a. 30%.
   b. 50%.
   c. 67%.
   d. 75%.

10. The safety net that exists after paying off a reverse mortgage loan provides for all of the following EXCEPT
    a. the ability to switch to a different reverse mortgage plan.
    b. starting a new plan.
    c. drawing on the funds that have been paid off.
    d. refinancing the home at no charge.

chapter six

Case Studies

The following Case Studies apply basic concepts from this course to "real-life" situations. Please read each Case Study carefully, then answer the questions and include your comments.

The following examples are hypothetical and no attempt has been made to depict actual experience from the files of senior homeowners.

| case study | **Chapter 1   Reverse Mortgages: Yesterday, Today, and Tomorrow** |

Case Study #1:

Lila and Steven Shaterivilli have lived in their home for 35 years. They were so proud when they paid off their mortgage loan five years ago and promised themselves they would never be in debt for their house again. Unfortunately, Steven recently had a severe heart attack and is unable to work or do any sort of physical exertion. Steven was a very successful custom-home builder for many years and was able to build an exceptional custom home for Lila and their three children. In fact, their home is worth twice the value of any other house in their small town. At this point in time, Steven and Lila are facing increased medical and living expenses and do not see any way out of their financial dilemma except to sell their beloved home. Their real estate broker neighbor, Michael Winston, has suggested they look into obtaining a reverse mortgage. Which of the following would be the best solution for Lila and Steven?

    a. Sell their house and move into an apartment.

    b. Apply for an FHA HECM reverse mortgage.

    c. Apply for a Fannie Mae Home Keeper® mortgage.

    d. Borrow money from their children to meet the new expenses.

Student Comments

Please provide your comments regarding the basic principle(s) addressed in this case study, and its relevance to the subject matter generally:

_____

_____

Case Study #2:

Jose and Olga Martinez are facing a severe financial dilemma. They saved for years before they were able to purchase their own home and now, only two years after the mortgage was paid off, they are afraid they will be forced to sell it and move into a small apartment. Jose is 75 and in fairly good health. Olga is only 62 but suffers from multiple sclerosis. As her condition worsens, they are faced with overwhelming medical expenses and also must pay for in-home care. A friend has suggested they look into obtaining an FHA Home Equity Conversion Mortgage, but Olga is very concerned about what would happen to her if Jose dies before she does. She is afraid that she then would be forced to sell the house to pay off the reverse mortgage loan and move at a time when her physical condition would be even worse. Which of the following characteristics of an FHA Home Equity Conversion Mortgage would be most important to Jose and Olga?

    a.   Both borrower and spouse must be at least 62.

    b.   The home must be an FHA-approved dwelling.

    c.   The home must be free of debt or nearly paid off.

    d.   The loan does not become due as long as one of the owners still occupies the home.

Student Comments

Please provide your comments regarding the basic principle(s) addressed in this case study, and its relevance to the subject matter generally:

---

    case study   **Chapter 2   A Guide to the Reverse Mortgage Plans**

Case Study #1:

Martha and Abe Stein have found that they are no longer able to pay their monthly expenses without some source of additional income. They both had worked for 30 years for a local department store and now receive small pensions, but their cost of living has increased far beyond their set income. Until last year, Abe was continuing to work part-time at the same store stocking shelves, but after suffering a minor back injury he is no longer able to continue. They recently attended a special program on reverse mortgages at their local synagogue and are considering whether a reverse mortgage could provide a solution to their financial needs. The program they attended was presented by Capital Savings Bank, a local savings association. The presenter explained that the particular reverse mortgage being offered by Capital Savings is for 20 years with no payment of the outstanding balance due until the end of the 20-year period. The $500 monthly payment that would be made to the Steins would solve their monthly cash flow problem, but they are concerned about making the payoff in 20 years. Abe is presently 65 years old and Martha just turned 62. What might be a better option for the Steins?

    a. Sell the house and move into a rental apartment.

    b. Move in with their oldest son and his family.

    c. Obtain a Fannie Mae Home Keeper® reverse mortgage.

    d. Obtain an FHA Home Equity Conversion Mortgage.

Student Comments

Please provide your comments regarding the basic principle(s) addressed in this case study, and its relevance to the subject matter generally:

_____

_____

_____

_____

Case Study #2:

Margaret and Stan Williams have been active members of the Calvary Baptist Church for many years and greatly enjoy participating in many of the charitable activities that their church organizes for less fortunate people. The Williamses are both in their early 60s and have been looking forward to when they can both draw full Social Security benefits. They have calculated that their combined Social Security draws will enable them to meet their monthly expenses, especially since their home is paid for. At that time, they will both quit their present jobs and devote more time to helping out with the different church activities. Last Sunday, their pastor announced a new program that Calvary Baptist is hoping to put into place at the beginning of next year. The plans are for a pre-school and after-school program for needy children whose parents both work. The children would be provided breakfast at the church before school and to and from the appropriate school. Upon their return to the church, snacks would be available in addition to planned games, sports activities, and time for study hall. The only problem is that there are not enough funds available both to provide for the program and to pay for staff. If the Williamses just could find a way to increase their monthly income, they would quit their "day jobs" now and provide full-time leadership for the new program at no cost to the church. Which one of the reverse mortgage plans would best help them achieve their goal?

    a. The tenure plan with regular monthly payments for life.

    b. The term plan with higher monthly payments for a set number of years.

    c. The line-of-credit plan, which allows for draws of different amounts at different times.

    d. The lump sum plan, which provides one large amount at the beginning.

Student Comments

Please provide your comments regarding the basic principle(s) addressed in this case study, and its relevance to the subject matter generally:

_____

_____

_____

_____

| case study | **Chapter 3   The Reverse Mortgage Loan** |

Case Study #1:

Mia and Tony Chen have determined that a reverse mortgage may be the answer to their prayers. After attending a Home Equity Conversion Mortgage counseling program offered by a local HUD-approved housing agency, they learned that they could use the equity that they have built up over the years in their home to supplement their income. The Chens have run a very successful dry-cleaning business for over 30 years but find that they are getting very tired of the mental and physical stress of owning and operating the shop. Between their savings and Social Security payments, they almost could meet their monthly expenses without the reverse mortgage, but they still have one daughter in college and one of their sons has just been accepted to medical school. The extra money from the reverse mortgage will provide just what they need in order to retire. They have received their Certificate of HECM Counseling and the next step will be to select a reverse mortgage lender. The HECM counselor referred them to various Web sites that list approved lenders, such as *www.hud.gov*, *www.fanniemae.com*, and *www.aarp.org*. Which of the following things to consider in selecting a lender should be the most important as the Chens make their selection?

a. Cost: the origination and servicing fees charged.
b. Experience: the number of HECM loans made each year.
c. Servicing: how administrative tasks are handled.
d. Commitment: membership in the National Reverse Mortgage Lenders Association.

Student Comments

Please provide your comments regarding the basic principle(s) addressed in this case study, and its relevance to the subject matter generally:

_____

_____

_____

_____

Case Study #2:

Richard and Kristen have enjoyed living in their small town in a rural area of Oklahoma for many years. They retired a few years ago and have been able to meet their monthly expenses up until this past year, when Richard suffered a stroke and now needs special medication and in-home care daily. They were referred to a HUD-approved counseling agency and after attending the session, they are very interested in obtaining an FHA Home Equity Conversion Mortgage as soon as possible. Their biggest concern is whether or not they will be able to obtain a large enough amount to help them meet their current needs. Property values in their area have been pretty stagnant for a number of years with little hope for much appreciation in the near future. The amount they can receive with a reverse mortgage is based on a percentage of the maximum claim amount (the value of the home at the time the property is sold to repay the loan). If the average house price in their area is $110,000 and their home is currently appraised for $115,000, what would be the maximum claim amount available to them?

- **a.** The FHA standard limit of $154,896.
- **b.** The current appraisal amount of $115,000.
- **c.** The average house price of $110,000.
- **d.** The local FHA limit of $104,500.

Student Comments

Please provide your comments regarding the basic principle(s) addressed in this case study, and its relevance to the subject matter generally:

_____

_____

_____

_____

case study | **Chapter 4   Reverse Mortgage Expenses, Fees, and Closing Costs**

Case Study #1:

When Jack and Judy Armstrong bought their first home back in 1957, Jack used his VA (Veterans Administration) eligibility. They were able to purchase the home with no money down and the seller paid all of the closing costs. In 1987, when Jack Jr. and his wife purchased their first home, they obtained a standard Fannie Mae conventional loan but the sellers agreed to pay 3 percent of the sales price towards the young couple's closing costs. Now Jack and Judy are retired and are considering a reverse mortgage using a line-of-credit plan in order to provide them extra funds from time to time to buy special gifts for their grandchildren, to travel, and to make some improvements to their home (which has been paid off for 15 years). As they go over the details of the plan with their chosen lender, Martin Kane of Citizens Bank, Jack asks how much of their closing costs will be paid by someone else. He tells Martin how it worked when he first bought the house and when their son obtained his first loan. When Martin tried to explain that with a reverse mortgage, all closing costs must be paid by the borrower, Jack became upset and considered forgetting the whole idea. Martin finally was able to calm down Jack (with some help from Judy). Martin could use all of the following explanations EXCEPT:

    a. The early VA loans deliberately were set up to assist veterans by requiring sellers to pay some of the closing costs and allowing sellers to pay all of the costs.

    b. Affordable loans, such as the Fannie Mae Community Homebuyer® used by Jack Jr. and his wife, allow the seller to pay up to 3 percent of the sales price to make it possible for more people to buy homes.

    c. Builders will often use the payment of all or part of closing costs as an incentive to buy their product rather than one down the street.

    d. It's your loan, pal, and you're the one who has to pay for it!

Student Comments

Please provide your comments regarding the basic principle(s) addressed in this case study, and its relevance to the subject matter generally:

_____

_____

_____

_____

Case Study #2:

When Sean and Mary O'Neil first considered obtaining a reverse mortgage, they thought they understood that instead of paying the bank, the bank now would send them money each month which would not be due and payable until they chose to leave the home. For example, if the bank sent them $500 each month, at the end of the year they would owe the bank $6000 ($500 x 12). At the end of 20 years they would owe $120,000. Unfortunately, there would hardly be any incentive for a bank to make such a loan. After further counseling, Sean and Mary realized that they would have to pay interest on the money borrowed plus other fees that would add up to the total balance due at the time the reverse mortgage loan was paid off. The total claim amount for their home is $150,000. Their homeowner insurance policy is $325 per year. Which of the following most likely would have the greatest impact on the total annual loan cost (TALC) for the $6000 they will receive?

    a. Adjustable interest rate

    b. Mortgage insurance premium

    c. Service fee

    d. Escrow for homeowner's insurance

Student Comments

Please provide your comments regarding the basic principle(s) addressed in this case study, and its relevance to the subject matter generally:

_____

_____

_____

_____

case study

Chapter 5   Tax Benefits and Treatments

Case Study #1:

Helen and Johnny Greenwood obtained an FHA Home Equity Conversion Mortgage eight years ago when they were both 64. Johnny had been a vice-president of a growing hi-tech firm for many years, but when the firm lost both of its major government contracts, they were forced to close down and Johnny was out of a job. Helen had also worked for the same company as a secretary, so their monthly income dropped to zero overnight. Since Helen had worked outside the home for only about six years, her Social Security benefits were small, and even with Johnny's benefits being at the full amount, they still could not meet their monthly expenses. They elected to take an HECM combination plan with a lump sum up front to help them cover their immediate needs and a small amount to be disbursed monthly. HECM was a lifesaver for them at the time, but they always felt badly about tying up all of the equity that they had built in their home for their own use and not being able to pass it along to their four children when they die. Five years ago Johnny started working as a Wal-Mart greeter and Helen went back to work part-time as a church secretary. With their two small salaries, their Social Security benefits, and the monthly payments on the HECM, they find that they are able to pay all of their bills and even start saving a small amount each month. Which of the following alternatives might appeal to them at this time?

    a.   Quit working and live off of the Social Security and HECM payments.

    b.   Use the HECM payments to buy a used RV and travel.

    c.   Start saving to pay off the HECM early and restore the equity in their home that could be left to the children in their estate.

    d.   Alternate sending the HECM payment to each child monthly.

Student Comments

Please provide your comments regarding the basic principle(s) addressed in this case study, and its relevance to the subject matter generally:

_____

_____

_____

_____

Resource List

■ AARP Publications:

A Profile of Older Americans (Stock #D996)—Summarizes major socioeconomic trends among older citizens.

Home-Made Money: A Consumer's Guide to Reverse Mortgages (Stock #D12894)— General overview of types of reverse mortgages.

Understanding Reverse Mortgages (Stock #D17329)—Also available in Spanish.

Reverse Mortgage Choices—A two-part videotape designed for consumers.

To order, write to:

AARP
Home Equity Information Center
601 E Street, N.W.
Washington, DC 20049
(202) 434-6042

■ Fannie Mae

Money From Home: A Guide to Understanding Reverse Mortgages—Provides comparison of FHA Home Equity Conversion Mortgage and Fannie Mae Home Keeper® reverse mortgage; available from Fannie Mae (call 1-800-7Fannie) or online at *www.fanniemae.com.*

■ Federal Trade Commission

Facts for Consumers—Reverse Mortgages—Available from Federal Trade Commission at Office of Consumer/Business Education, Washington, DC 20580

■ HUD

HUD Handbook 4330.1 REV-5, "Home Equity Conversion Mortgages"—Good for technical reference; available through HUD or online at *www.hudclips.org*.

■ Internet Resources

www.aarp.org—American Association of Retired Persons; general information on senior citizens rights and opportunities.

www.aarp.org/revmort—contains the most recent online version of "Home Made Money."

www.hud.gov—Department of Housing and Urban Development; click on "Senior Citizens," then "Reverse Mortgages for Seniors."

www.fanniemae.com—Click on "Homepath," then "Find a Mortgage," then "Reverse Mortgages for Seniors," then "Money From Home."

www.irs.gov—Source for information on tax-free gifts and other tax benefits.

www.reversemortgage.org—National Reverse Mortgage Lenders Association; provides general information plus list of approved lenders.

www.reverse.org—National Center for Home Equity Conversion Web site; an independent, not-for-profit organization established in 1981 to educate consumers about reverse mortgages.

401(k) A retirement plan funded by both employer and employee.

Adjustable Rate Mortgage (ARM) A mortgage loan in which the interest rate is subject to change at specified adjustment periods based on a current financing index.

Annuity An insurance company plan that provides monthly cash advances.

Appraisal A professional opinion of a property's market value.

Appreciation An increase in the value of a property.

Cap A limitation on how much an interest rate may increase in any given adjustment period on an adjustable rate mortgage.

Clear Title When there are no liens or legal questions regarding ownership of a property.

Closing Also referred to as "settlement"; a time when all legal documents are signed that originate a mortgage loan and/or purchase a property.

Closing Costs Costs paid by a borrower at closing; may include origination fee, title insurance, appraisal, survey, attorney fees, and prepaid items such as insurance and taxes.

Collateral Provides the right to obtain title to a property in case a borrower defaults on loan payments.

Contingency A condition stated in a contract that must be met before settlement.

Deed of Trust A financing instrument used to establish property as collateral for a loan; allows for a trustee to exercise power-of-sale in case of default by the borrower.

Deferred Payment Loan A type of reverse mortgage loan granted by local government agencies for the repair or improvement of a home.

Depreciation A decline in the value of a property.

Equity The difference between the market value and the outstanding liens on a property.

Escrow Funds Money held by the lender to pay taxes and insurance on behalf of the borrower.

Expected Average Interest Rate A fixed rate used to establish the amount of money available to a borrower at closing on a HECM (not the same as the interest rate charged on the outstanding loan balance); equals the ten-year rate for U.S. Treasury securities, plus a margin.

Fannie Mae Stockholder-owned company that purchases mortgage loans from local lenders; primary purchaser of FHA insured Home Equity Conversion Mortgage (HECM) loans.

Fannie Mae Loan Limit Established annually based on current housing prices and loan amounts; limits the amount of value used to determine cash advances on reverse mortgages.

Federal Income Tax Paid annually to the Internal Revenue Service; although mortgage interest is deductible for tax purposes, it may not be claimed on a reverse mortgage until the mortgage is paid off.

FHA Federal Housing Administration. Part of the Department of Housing and Urban Development (HUD); insures HECM loans.

FHA Loan Limits Maximum loan amounts allowed for FHA mortgage loans; set annually based on average house prices by county or city; limits how much of a home's value can be used to determine loan advances for HECM.

FHA Mortgage Insurance Charged to borrowers on HECMs to provide a pool of funds that protects the lender in case of default by borrowers; also provides assurance that payments will be made to borrowers in case of bankruptcy or default by lender.

Forward Mortgage Type of mortgage used to purchase a property. The total amount is distributed at the origination of mortgage; monthly payments decrease the principal balance due.

HECM Home Equity Conversion Mortgage; reverse mortgage insured by FHA.

Home Equity Loan Loan that allows the borrower to receive funds based on the value of the property; requires monthly payments and borrower qualification.

Home Inspection Inspection made by a professional inspector to determine the condition of the property.

Home Keeper® Fannie Mae's reverse mortgage plan.

Homeowner's Property Tax Tax levied by local government based on the assessed value of property.

Homeowner Insurance Insurance that protects both the lender and homeowner from physical damage to the property and provides liability coverage.

HUD Department of Housing and Urban Development; responsibilities include operation of FHA and oversight of Fannie Mae.

Interest A fee charged by a lender for the use of money.

IRA Individual Retirement Account; provides tax benefits for savings.

IRS Tax-Free Gifts Internal Revenue Service policy allowing anyone to give $11,000 to another person annually with no tax consequences.

Lien A financial claim against a property (like a mortgage).

Living Educational Legacy Providing funds for education during time the senior person is alive instead of as part of an estate distributed after death.

Loan-to-Value Percentage relationship between the amount of the loan and the market value of the property; i.e., 80% LTV = $80,000 loan on $100,000 valued property.

Loan Balance Amount owed to the lender including principal and interest plus all other fees incurred as part of a reverse mortgage.

Lump Sum Single loan advance of the total amount available for a reverse mortgage at closing.

Margin Amount added to the U.S. Treasury rate to determine initial and current interest rates.

Maximum Claim Amount The lesser of a property's appraised value or the maximum loan amount allowed by FHA in the local area.

Mortgage Legal document establishing property as collateral for a loan.

Mortgage-Backed Securities A group of similar loans purchased by Fannie Mae and packaged to be sold on the open market.

Mortgage Insurance (MIP or PMI) A fee charged to a borrower to protect the lender in case of default; FHA HECM insurance is called MIP (mortgage insurance premium), Fannie Mae Home Keeper® insurance is called PMI (private mortgage insurance).

NRMLA National Reverse Mortgage Lenders Association; provides information and approved lenders for reverse mortgages.

Origination Fee Administrative charge for the processing of a mortgage loan.

Periodic Statements Statements provided by the lender to the borrower each month showing the current status of the reverse mortgage with the total balance due to date.

Points One point is usually one percent of the loan amount; it may be charged by the lender to reduce the interest rate.

Principal The actual amount of money distributed to the borrower; is gradually reduced on forward mortgage and gradually increases with a reverse mortgage.

Proprietary Reverse Mortgage One provided by a private lender that is not insured by FHA.

Recording Fees Fees charged by local jurisdictions for recording of documents.

Reverse Mortgage A loan against equity in the home that provides cash advances to the borrower and is not repaid until the borrower either dies or leaves the property.

Servicing Fee Fee charged by a lender after closing for performing administrative functions related to the reverse mortgage loan.

Settlement See Closing.

Social Security Benefits Retirement payments made to senior citizens based on age and/or disability.

Special Assessments Assessments made to individual homeowners by local jurisdictions for improvements to the property; i.e., sidewalks, streetlights, curbs.

Student Loan Low-interest rate government-insured loans made to students.

Survey Drawing showing boundaries, improvements, easements, and/or encroachments on property.

Tax Reporting Service Service provided to lenders assuring that all property taxes are timely paid.

Tenure Plan Reverse mortgage with monthly payments to the borrower as long as at least one homeowner remains in the property; the balance is due when the property is no longer the borrower's principal residence.

Term Plan Same as the tenure plan except that payments to the borrower stop after a set number of years.

Title Insurance Purchased by the borrower; protects both lender and homeowner against past title defects.

Total Annual Loan Cost (TALC) The projected annual average cost of a reverse mortgage including all itemized costs such as interest, taxes, insurance, and servicing fees.

Total Finance Charges The sum of all accrued interest plus mortgage insurance premiums paid each year and reported annually to the borrower.

Uninsured Reverse Mortgage A proprietary reverse mortgage that becomes due and payable on a specific date.

Chapter 1 Review Questions Answers

1. b. Federal Home Loan Bank. The concept of a reverse mortgage was conceived by the Federal Home Loan Bank in 1979.

2. c. Purchasing loans from lenders providing reverse mortgage loans. Fannie Mae began purchasing FHA reverse mortgages in 1989, which provides additional funds for the lender to make more reverse mortgage loans.

3. d. Home Keeper®. Fannie Mae was so impressed with the FHA Home Equity Conversion Mortgage that it created its own program in 1996.

4. c. HECM. The HUD-designed, FHA-insured reverse mortgage is called a Home Equity Conversion Mortgage and started as an experimental program in 1989.

5. b. 62 years old. One of the requirements for all types of reverse mortgages is that both homeowners be at least 62 years old.

6. d. The borrowers must be financially qualified by the lender. There are no financial requirements for the borrowers with a reverse mortgage loan.

7. b. Both Joe and Mary no longer remain in the home. Reverse mortgage loans are not repaid until the last surviving homeowner leaves the home.

8. a. Principal balance goes up, equity goes down. The reverse mortgage loan is just the opposite of a forward mortgage loan where the principal balance decreases and the equity in the home increases.

9. d. $1350 principal plus interest and other charges. Each month, the principal payment of $450 is added to the total loan balance plus all accrued interest, mortgage insurance, and servicing fees.

10. d. Insured Plan. The four types of plans are the tenure, term, line of credit, and lump sum. Plans may be insured by FHA but there is no plan called the insured plan.

Chapter 2 Review Questions Answers

1. b. Monthly advances for life, or until the homeowners leave the home.

2. b. Deed of Trust or Mortgage. The use of either of these financing instruments used to provide collateral for the reverse mortgage loan varies by state.

3. d. Financial ability of the homeowners. Since there are no monthly payments to be made to the lender, there is no requirement for financial ability to repay on the part of the homeowner.

4. a. Sends a check to the homeowners or makes a deposit to their account. Under the tenure plan, monthly payments of a predetermined amount are made to the homeowners, either by check or bank deposit.

5. d. Mary's monthly advances from the lender will continue until she either dies or decides to leave the home. One of the primary benefits of a reverse mortgage is that payments will continue as long as one of the homeowners remains living in the property.

6. b. Larger monthly advances for the specified term of years. Because of the likelihood that payments will be made to the homeowner for a much

shorter period of time than with a tenure plan, the monthly payments will be larger.

7. c. Time period for which payments are desired. All reverse mortgages are based on the location, value, and equity of the home, plus the age of the youngest borrower and the interest rate at time of closing. The additional factor for a term plan is the time period requested for payments to be made.

8. b. Helen's husband has terminal Lou Gehrig's disease and needs hospice care. Presumably, Helen will need a larger sum of money for a shorter period of time rather than an increase in her monthly income for life.

9. c. Funds are withdrawn only when needed. The line-of-credit plan allows for withdrawals as needed for homeowners that do not need an increase in their monthly income but wish to have funds available for special needs or wants.

10. b As money is withdrawn. Interest is only charged each month for the total principal amount drawn to date.

11. d. The lender may force sale of the property if it is vacated for more than one year. The reverse mortgage loan agreement will generally specify that the lender must be notified if the homeowners plan to be away from the property for more than two months; an absence of a year could require the property to be sold.

12. c. Combination lump sum and tenure plan. Both FHA and Fannie Mae offer combination plans that allow the borrower to combine receiving one large lump sum at closing plus regular monthly payments for life.

13. c. $22,000. The IRS will allow each of the grandparents to make an annual gift of $11,000 to each girl with no tax consequences.

14. a. The college will have to accept Tim regardless of his grades. Robert may provide the financial capability for Tim to go to college; passing the academic entrance requirements will remain Tim's responsibility.

15. b. Sale of their current home plus the ability to secure a reverse mortgage loan on the new property. Using a reverse mortgage for the purchase of a new home is a very complicated process and must be handled carefully. It is essential that any offer to purchase include two contingencies: one for the sale of their current home, and one for the ability to secure a new reverse mortgage.

Chapter 3 Review Questions Answers

1. c. Locate a HUD-approved reverse mortgage housing counselor. Counseling will be required for both FHA and Fannie Mae reverse mortgages plus the counseling session will also discuss other alternatives to solve financial dilemmas.

2. a. Two hours. FHA requires a two hour counseling session before applying for a home equity conversion mortgage.

3. b. Choose a lender with experience in reverse mortgage loans. Experience will make the process go much smoother and is more important than costs.

4. c. Line-of-credit plan. With all other plans, the total amount available is established at the time of closing. The line-of-credit reverse mortgage will increase slightly until all available funds are withdrawn.

5. b. Current FHA loan limit for that geographic area. The amount available is based on a percentage of the market value of the property at the time of closing, but is subject to FHA loan limits which vary by area.

6. a. Current Fannie Mae loan limit. The amount available is based on a percentage of the market value of the home at the time of closing subject to current Fannie Mae conventional loan limits.

7. c. Interest on an HECM is calculated weekly and must be paid each month.

8. a. How the funds are to be used by the borrower. There is no limitation on how the borrowers can use the funds received through a reverse mortgage.

9. b. 13%. An annually adjusted HECM is limited to no more than 5% over the starting rate for the life of the loan.

10. d. Nothing. Even though the lender may require that money be advanced for the credit report and appraisal at the time of application, these costs can be reimbursed at closing from reverse mortgage loan proceeds.

Chapter 4 Review Questions Answers

1. c. Four to six weeks. It generally takes a little longer to process a reverse mortgage loan than a loan for the purchase of property, even though there are no qualifying requirements for the borrower.

2. d. The senior borrowers will have to pay all of the closing costs but the costs can be rolled into the loan. All closing costs must be paid by the borrower but the costs can be paid at closing through funds received through the reverse mortgage loan.

3. d. Maintenance reserve. Although arrangements could be made between the borrower and the lender to establish a maintenance reserve, this would not be normal closing cost.

4. d. Borrower's life insurance. Although it is possible for a borrower to purchase life insurance with funds received from a reverse mortgage, this would not an allowable closing cost.

5. a. If they stay in the property for 20 years, the reverse mortgage will have been less expensive. If the $7,500 is spread out over 20 years it will represent a much smaller percentage of the cost of the total reverse mortgage than if it is only spread over a smaller number of years.

6. c. Higher than for a typical forward mortgage, but lower than for a proprietary reverse mortgage. The costs for a FHA HECM are slightly higher than for a typical forward mortgage, but are less than for a proprietary reverse mortgage offered by a private lender.

7. d. The total debt may not exceed the value of the home, no matter how long the seniors live. One of the primary benefits of the FHA-insured HECM is that the borrowers will never be liable for any shortfall between the amount the lender receives when the home is sold and the total loan balance due.

8. c. Identify any outstanding student or other government loans. Even though there are no financial requirements for the borrowers, the lender wants to be sure there are no outstanding amounts due to the government.

9. d. To pay for preparation of the deed granting title to the property. Title insurance protects both the borrower and the lender from any future claims to the property arising from the past; it does not pay for preparation of the deed.

10. d. Title insurance monthly premiums. Title insurance is a one-time cost, paid at closing. Interest, mortgage insurance, and servicing fees are added each month to the total loan balance.

Chapter 5 Review Questions Answers

1. c. The interest paid on a reverse mortgage is deductible in the year it is charged. The IRS does not allow for interest to be claimed until it is actually paid which in the case of a reverse mortgage, is at the time the property is sold and the loan paid off.

2. b. The homeowner must pay property taxes out-of-pocket each year. Although the property tax may be paid annually at the option of the home-owner, it can also be included in an escrow account held by the lender and charged to the total loan balance each month.

3. c. Subscribe to a tax reporting service. Because the consequences of a tax sale forced by delinquent taxes would be devastating to both homeowner and lender, the lender may subscribe to this service that may be charged back to the homeowner.

4. d. Accrued monthly service fees. Monthly service fees cannot be treated as federal income tax deductions at the time of sale or any time. Accrued interest and accrued mortgage insurance premiums are added together for total interest paid and the sum is deductible for federal tax purposes if an itemized return is filed. Also, home property tax and special improvement taxes paid in the year of sale may be deducted.

5. b. Jack and Marie file an itemized tax return. Federal tax deductions for both interest and property taxes can only be taken in the year that the loan is paid off and only if the borrowers file an itemized tax return.

6. c. A tax professional. Although it is important for a real estate professional to be knowledgeable about tax issues in general, specific issues for individuals should always be handled by a tax professional.

7. d. Should be carefully researched before purchasing. Even the interest paid on an annuity may seem attractive, there are still certain risks that must be addressed before a homeowner should use reverse mortgage funds to purchase an annuity.

8. c. The fact the reverse mortgage will diminish the value of an estate should be discussed openly with members of the family who will be affected. Family members are strongly urged to attend the reverse mortgage counseling sessions so that the effect on the seniors' estate will be clearly defined.

9. c. 67% This high rate of homeownership emphasizes the amount of equity that is available as more people enter retirement age.

10. d. Refinancing the home at no charge. After paying off the reverse mortgage loan debt, the homeowners have the option of either creating a new plan or drawing on funds that have been paid off; there is no refinancing involved.

Chapter 6 Case Studies

Chapter 1 Case Study #1:

c. Applying for a Fannie Mae Home Keeper® reverse mortgage would be the best solution since the FHA HECM would be limited to local maximum loan amounts, which most likely would be below the value of their property.

Chapter 1 Case Study #2:

d. Because FHA insurance provides that payments will continue as long as one of the owners occupies the home as a principal residence, Olga would have the comfort of knowing that she could continue living in the home and receive the same payment each month to help with her medical expenses and in-home care.

Chapter 2 Case Study #1:

d. The Steins' best option would be an FHA HECM reverse mortgage. The FHA mortgage insurance guarantees that the monthly payments will continue as long as at least one of them still lives in the home, even if the total balance due should exceed the maximum claim amount at the time the property is eventually sold.

Chapter 2 Case Study #2:

b. Since the term plan is set for a specific number of years, the monthly payments are larger than those for the tenure plan. Since the Williamses need to provide monthly income for themselves for only a few years until they can draw the maximum Social Security amount, the term plan would be the best choice. A line-of-credit also could work but would require more bookkeeping. The lump sum would require more discipline to spread the money out over the time needed.

Chapter 3 Case Study #1:

b. Experience is the key factor. Just as the Chens could show that their 30 years of experience in the dry-cleaning business is more important than the cost to clean a suit, the way their bookkeeping is handled, or their commitment to the local Chamber of Commerce, the same is true for the reverse mortgage lender. Costs do not vary much from one lender to the next, servicing is important but is tied into a background of experience, and commitment is wonderful but meaningless if this is the first reverse mortgage the lender has ever done!

Chapter 3 Case Study #2:

d. The maximum claim amount is determined by the local FHA maximum loan amount, which represents 95 percent of the average house price for the area. ($110,000 x 95% = $104,500)

Chapter 4 Case Study #1:

d. Although it is true that with a reverse mortgage there is no other party that has a vested interest in paying closing costs for the senior borrower, a more rational approach such as those suggested in 1, 2, and 3 probably would be much more effective.

Chapter 4 Case Study #2:

a. Assuming an average interest rate of 6.5 percent, interest for the year would be $390; mortgage insurance is 0.5 percent of $6,000 or $30; service fees average $30 per month or $360 per year; and the escrow for homeowner's insurance would be $325.

Chapter 5 Case Study #1:

c. Once people have been able to get over their immediate financial crises, they often find that they would like to rebuild their estate in order to leave something to their children when they die. A few years of employment often can pay back the reverse mortgage balance due and restore the equity in the home. The equity always could be considered as a reserve in case they should encounter financial needs in the future.